THE PROBLEM OF ANXIETY

SIGMUND FREUD

The
PROBLEM
of
ANXIETY

*Translated from the German
by Henry Alden Bunker, M.D.*

THE
PSYCHOANALYTIC QUARTERLY
PRESS

AND

W·W·NORTON & COMPANY, INC.
70 Fifth Avenue, New York

First Edition

---

*Authorized translation from the original German version
entitled* HEMMING, SYMPTOM UND ANGST

PRINTED IN THE UNITED STATES OF AMERICA
FOR THE PUBLISHERS BY THE VAIL-BALLOU PRESS

Contents

v

Translator's Foreword

I wish to express my great indebtedness to my friends and colleagues, Dr. Charles O. Fiertz and Dr. Bertram D. Lewin, for the unstinting assistance they have given me in the many and valuable suggestions which they, together also with Dr. Dorian Feigenbaum and Dr. Sandor Rado, have been kind enough to make—suggestions which, as I am gratefully aware, are responsible for much of whatever merit this translation may possess. Acknowledgment is no less due to Dr. Feigenbaum, Editor-in-Chief of *The Psychoanalytic Quarterly,* in that it was he who conceived the idea, and made possible the accomplishment, of a new translation of one of Freud's major works.

HENRY ALDEN BUNKER

September 15, 1936

THE PROBLEM OF ANXIETY

A Definition of Inhibition and Symptom

O UR verbal usage permits us, in describing pathological phenomena, to distinguish between inhibitions and symptoms, although without attaching very much importance to the distinction. If we did not encounter cases of which we are forced to say that they exhibit only inhibitions, without any symptoms, and if we did not wish to know the reason for this, we should scarcely think it worth while to demarcate the concepts "inhibition" and "symptom."

The two concepts are not rooted in the same soil. Inhibition relates specifically to function and does not necessarily denote something pathological; a normal restriction or reduction of a function may also be termed an inhibition of it. To speak of a symptom, on the other hand, is tantamount to indicating a morbid process. Thus an inhibition may also be a symptom. Our habits of speech are such, then, as cause us to speak of an inhibition when a simple reduction of function is present, of a symptom when it is a question of an unusual alteration of function or of a new modality thereof. In many cases it seems to be perfectly arbitrary whether one emphasizes the positive or the negative aspect of a pathological process, whether one terms its result a symptom or an inhibition. All this is of little real interest, however, and the way in which we have formulated our problem proves to be a rather unfruitful one.

Since inhibition is by definition so intimately bound up with function, it is but a short step to the idea of investigating the various ego functions with reference to the forms in which disorder of these functions is manifested in the various neurotic affections. We select for this comparative study the following: the sexual function, eating, locomotion, and vocation.

(a) The sexual function is subject to a great multiplicity of disturbances, the majority of which have the character of simple inhibitions. These are grouped together as psychic impotence. The execution of the sex act presupposes a very complicated sequence of events, any one of which may be the locus of disturbance. The principal loci of inhibition in men are the following: a turning aside of the libido at the initiation of the act (psychic unpleasure (*Unlust*)), absence of physical preparedness (non-erectibility), abbreviation of the act (ejaculatio præcox), which may equally well be described as a positive symptom, suspension of the act before its natural culmination (absence of ejaculation), the non-occurrence of the psychic effect (of the pleasure sensation of orgasm). Other disturbances result from the association with the sexual function of specific conditions of a perverse or fetishistic character.

We cannot long escape noting a relationship which inhibition bears to anxiety. Many inhibitions are an obvious renunciation of function, because the exercise of the function would give rise to anxiety. Outright dread of the sexual function is frequent in women; we catalogue this with hysteria, as we do also the defensive symptom of disgust which arises originally as a reaction following upon the sexual act as passively experienced, but later appears in relation to the mere idea of it. A great many compulsive acts likewise plainly serve as a precaution and an assurance against sexual experience, and are therefore phobic in their character.

This does not add much to our understanding,

however; one sees merely that the most varied means are employed to impair function, as: (1) the mere turning aside of libido, which seems most easily to produce what we call pure inhibition; (2) impairment of the execution of the function; (3) the rendering it difficult through the imposition of special conditions, and its modification through diverting it to other aims; (4) its prevention by means of precautionary measures; (5) its discontinuance by the development of anxiety, when the initiation of the function can no longer be prevented; finally, (6) a subsequent reaction of protest against the act and a desire to undo it if it has actually been carried out.

(*b*) The most frequent disturbance of the nutritive function is anorexia through withdrawal of libido. Increased desire to eat is also not infrequent; there is also a compulsion to eat, motivated by a fear of starvation, which has been little studied. As an hysterical defense against eating, the symptom of vomiting is familiar. Refusal to eat as a reaction to anxiety belongs among the psychotic patterns of behavior (delusions of poisoning).

(*c*) Locomotion is inhibited in many neurotic states by antipathy to walking and weakness in walking; the hysterical disability makes use of paralysis of the motor apparatus or creates a specific suspension of this one function of the latter (abasia). Particularly characteristic are the difficulties of locomotion brought about by the interpolation of definite conditions as prerequisites, the non-fulfillment of which evokes anxiety (phobia).

(*d*) Inhibition in the field of occupation, which so often becomes a matter of treatment as an isolated symptom, is evidenced in diminished pleasure in work, or in its poor execution, or in such reactive manifestations as fatigue (vertigo, vomiting) if the subject forces himself to go on working. Hysteria compels the suspension of work by producing paralysis of organs and functions, the existence of which is incompatible with the carrying on of work. The compulsion neurosis interferes with work by a continuous distraction of the attention and by loss of time in the form of procrastination and repetition.

We might extend this survey to include still other functions, but we should not expect to profit by so doing. We should not get beyond a mere scratching of the surface in this way. Let us therefore decide upon a formulation which will leave the concept of inhibition with as little of the mysterious about it as possible. Inhibition is the expression of a *functional limitation of the ego*—a limitation which may have a large variety of causes. Many of the mechanisms of this renunciation of function, and its general trend, are well known.

In the case of certain particular inhibitions the trend expressed is rather easily recognized. When playing the piano, writing, and even walking are made the subject of neurotic inhibition, analysis reveals as the basis thereof an excessive erotization of the organ involved in the function in question, the fingers and the feet. We have obtained the impression that as a rule the ego function of an organ is impaired whenever its erogeneity, its sexual significance, is increased. The organ then behaves—if we may hazard a somewhat scurrilous metaphor—like a cook who refuses to stay in the kitchen because the master of the house has embarked upon an affair with her. If writing—which consists in allowing a fluid to flow out from a tube upon a piece of white paper—has acquired the symbolic meaning of coitus, or if walking has become a symbolic substitute for stamping upon the body of Mother Earth, then both writing and walking will be abstained from, because it is as though forbidden sexual behavior were thereby being indulged in. The ego renounces these functions proper to it in order not to have to undertake a fresh effort of repression, *in order to avoid a conflict with the id.*

Other inhibitions evidently subserve a desire for self-punishment, as for example not infrequently those in the sphere of vocational activity. The ego dares not do certain things because they would bring an advantage and a success which the strict superego has forbidden. Thereupon the ego renounces these activities also, *in order not to become involved in conflict with the superego.*

The more general inhibitions of the ego follow a simple mechanism of another character. When the ego is occupied with a psychic task of special difficulty, as for example by mourning, a wholesale suppression of affect, or by the necessity for holding constantly mounting sexual fantasies in check, it becomes so impoverished with respect to the energy available to it that it is driven to restrict its expenditure in many places at the same time, like a speculator who has tied up his money in his various enterprises. An instructive example of such an intense but temporary general inhibition I was able to observe in a patient with compulsion neurosis who was overcome by a paralyzing fatigue of one to several days' duration on occasions which obviously should have provoked an outburst of rage.

From this point of departure there must be found a path to the understanding of generalized inhibition whereby we may characterize the depressive states and the most severe of these, psychotic depression.

One may therefore say of inhibitions, in fine, that they represent a limitation and restriction of ego functions, either precautionary or resulting from an impoverishment of energy. It is now easy to see wherein an inhibition differs from a symptom. A symptom can no longer be described as a process taking place either in or around the ego.

Symptom Formation

T HE fundamentals of neurotic symptom formation have long been studied and have been
laid down in incontestable fashion, one may hope.
Symptoms are supposed to be an indication of and
substitute for an unachieved instinctual gratification; they are, that is, a result of a process of repression. Repression proceeds from the ego, which, possibly at the command of the superego, does not wish
to be a party to an instinct cathexis originating in
the id. Through repression the ego accomplishes
the exclusion from consciousness of the idea which
was the carrier of the unwelcome impulse. Analysis
frequently demonstrates that the idea has been re-
tained as an unconscious formation. So far the
matter is clear enough, but presently we encounter
unsolved difficulties.

The description we have given heretofore of the
process involved in repression has expressly emphasized the result it achieves in excluding something

from consciousness, but has left other points open to doubt. The question arises as to the fate of the instinctual impulse generated in the id which strives for gratification. The answer has been an indirect one; it was to the effect that through repression the pleasure that was to be expected in gratification was converted into unpleasure (*Unlust*); whereupon one was confronted by the problem of how unpleasure can be the result of the gratification of an instinct. We hope we shall clarify the situation if we lay it down definitely that in consequence of repression the excitation arising in the id altogether fails of discharge: the ego succeeds in inhibiting or deflecting it. Thus the riddle of the "transformation of affect" in repression disappears. But we have thereby conceded to the ego the ability to exert so far-reaching an influence upon the processes taking place in the id, and have now to learn to understand the way in which this surprising manifestation of power becomes possible to the ego.

I believe that the ego possesses this influence by virtue of its intimate relationship to the perceptual system, a relationship which determines its very being and has become the basis of its differentiation from the id. The function of this system, which

we have labelled *Pcpt-Cs,*[1] is connected with the
phenomenon of consciousness; it is the recipient
of stimuli not only from without but likewise from
within, and through the medium of the sensations
of pleasure and unpleasure which reach it there-
from it attempts to direct all psychic activity in
accordance with the pleasure principle. We like
to conceive of the ego as powerless against the id,
but when the ego struggles against an instinctual
force in the id, it merely needs to give a signal of
distress to attain its purpose through the aid of the
all but omnipotent pleasure principle. If we consider this situation as an isolated phenomenon for
a moment, we may illustrate it by an example from
another field. In a given community a certain
clique opposes a political measure, the passage of
which would accord with the wishes of the majority. This minority then assumes control of the
press, influences sovereign "public opinion" in this
way, and thus succeeds in preventing the passage
of the projected measure.

But this formulation gives rise to further questions. What is the source of the energy which is
used to create the signal of distress? The answer
is indicated by the notion that the defense against

[1] See *The Ego and the Id,* Chapter II.—TRANSLATOR'S NOTE.

an undesirable endopsychic process might take place after the pattern of defense against an external stimulus—that the ego employs the same measures of defense against an internal as against an external danger. In the case of external danger the organism makes an attempt at flight; it first withdraws its libidinal cathexis from the perception of the danger; it later learns that a more effective measure consists in carrying out such muscular activity as will make impossible the perception of the danger even when the danger is not denied—in other words, it learns to withdraw from the area of danger. Repression is the equivalent of an attempt at flight of this kind. The ego withdraws (preconscious) cathexis from the instinct representative which is to be repressed and utilizes it in the release of unpleasure (anxiety). The problem of how anxiety arises in repression is clearly not a simple one; but at all events one may justifiably hold to the view that the ego is the real locus of anxiety, and reject the earlier conception that the cathectic energy of the repressed impulse automatically becomes converted into anxiety. If I formerly so expressed myself, I was giving a phenomenological description and not a metapsychological statement of the matter.

From the foregoing there arises the further question as to how it is possible from an economic standpoint that a mere process of withdrawal or discharge, such as in the case of the retreat of the preconscious ego-cathexis, should give rise to unpleasure or anxiety, which according to our supposition can only be the result of an increased cathexis. I would reply that such a causation is not to be explained on an economic basis; anxiety is not created *de novo* in repression, but is reproduced as an affective state in accordance with a memory picture already present. With the further question as to the origin of this anxiety—and as to that of affects in general—we leave behind the undisputed field of psychology, however, and enter the borderland of physiology. Affective states are incorporated into the life of the psyche as precipitates of primal traumatic experiences, and are evoked in similar situations like memory symbols. I believe I was not wrong in regarding these states as the equivalents of hysterical attacks developed later and individually, and in considering the former as the normal prototypes of the latter. In man and in creatures related to him the act of birth, as the initial individual experience of anxiety, seems to have lent characteristic features to the expression of the affect of anxiety. We ought not to place too great value upon this relationship, however, nor in its recognition overlook the fact that an affective symbol for the danger situation is a biological necessity and would have been created in any case. I likewise consider it inadmissible to assume that in every outbreak of anxiety something occurs in the psyche which is analogous to a reproduction of the birth situation. It is not even certain whether hysterical seizures, which are originally traumatic reproductions of this kind, retain this characteristic permanently.

I have elsewhere stated that the majority of repressions with which we have to do in therapeutic work are instances of *subsequential* repression (*Nachdrängen*). They presuppose *primal* repressions (*Urverdrängungen*) of an earlier date which exercise over the more recent situation their gravitative influence. But far too little is as yet known concerning this hinterground and these primary stages of repression. One easily runs the risk of overestimating the rôle of the superego in repression. At the present time it is impossible to decide whether the erecting of the superego perhaps creates the demarcation between primal and subsequential repression. At all events, the first, and very intense, attacks of anxiety occur prior to the differentiation of the superego. It is entirely reasonable to suppose that quantitative factors, such as a stimulus of excessive strength, with the failure of the safety device protective against too powerful stimuli (*Reizschutz*), are the most direct causation of primal repression.

The mention of this safeguard reminds us that repression takes place in two distinct situations, namely, when an unwelcome instinctual impulse is aroused by an external perception, and when the impulse arises internally without such provocation. We shall return later to this distinction. Defense against stimuli occurs only against external stimuli, however, not against internal instinctual demands.

As long as we pay sole attention to the attempt at flight on the part of the ego, we do not even come close to the question of how symptoms are formed. Symptoms result from the injuring of the instinctual impulse through repression. If by means of a signal of distress the ego attains its object of completely suppressing the instinctual impulse, we have no intimation as to how this happens. We learn something about it only from the cases in which repression is more or less unsuccessful. Then it appears, in general, that the instinctual impulse, despite repression, has found a substitute satisfaction, but one which is greatly crippled, displaced, or inhibited. It is not even any longer recognizable as a gratification. If a substitute satisfaction is achieved, pleasure is not experienced, but instead the achieving of this substitute satisfaction has acquired the character of a compulsion. But in the degradation of the process of gratification to the status of a symptom, repression manifests its power in still another respect. Whenever possible, the substitutive process is kept from being carried out by the motor apparatus; and when this does not succeed, it must use itself up in an alteration of the subject's own body, without encroachment upon the environment; it is not permitted to be transformed into action. As I understand it, in repression the ego functions under the influence of external reality and therefore excludes the result of the substitutive process from this reality.

The ego controls the entrance into consciousness as well as the passage into activity directed to the environment; in repression it exerts its power at both places. The instinct representative experiences the one, the instinctual impulse itself the other side of the ego's manifestation of authority. So it becomes pertinent to ask how this appreciation of the might of the ego harmonizes with the description which we outlined in *The Ego and the*

Id of the position occupied by this same ego. We there described the dependence of the ego upon the id as well as upon the superego, and unmasked its impotence and apprehensiveness towards both, and also the superiority which it maintains so arduously. This point of view has since produced a number of reverberations in psychoanalytic literature. Many opinions have forcibly emphasized the weakness of the ego in relation to the id, of the rational against the demonic in us, and are on the point of making this pronouncement into a pillar of a psychoanalytic *Weltanschauung*. But ought not insight into the *modus operandi* of repression to restrain the analyst, of all persons, from such an extreme of partisanship?

I am not at all in favor of elaborating *Weltanschauungen*. Let that be left to the philosophers, who avowedly do not find the journey of life practicable without a Baedeker of this kind, which supplies information about everything. Let us accept with all humility the disdain with which the philosophers look down upon us from the vantage point of their more elevated indigence. Since we too cannot disown our narcissistic pride, we will seek consolation in the consideration that all these "guides to life" quickly become obsolete, that it is precisely our shortsightedly circumscribed efforts which make new editions of them necessary, and that even the most up-to-date of these Baedekers are attempts to take the place of the old Catechism, so handy and so complete. We know full well how little light science has been able to throw upon the riddles of this world; all the bombinations of the philosophers cannot alter that fact, but only patient and unremitting work, which subordinates everything to the single demand for certitude, can at long last bring about a change in this respect. When the wayfarer whistles in the dark, he may be disavowing his timidity, but he does not see any the more clearly for doing so.

The Ego

To RETURN to the problem of the ego: The apparent contradiction of which we have been speaking arises from the fact that we take abstractions too rigidly, and from out of a complicated state of affairs we pick now one aspect and now another exclusively. The separation of the ego from the id seems justified, indeed is forced upon us, by certain findings. Yet on the other hand the ego is identical with the id, is only a specially differentiated portion of it. If in our thinking we contrast this portion with the whole, or if an actual disjunction of the two has come about, then the weakness of this ego becomes evident. If, however, the ego remains one with the id and indistinguishable from it, then it is its strength that is apparent. The same with the relation of the ego to the superego: as regards many situations they are one and the same; as a rule we can distinguish them only when a state of tension, a conflict between them, has arisen. In the case of repression the fact of crucial importance is that the ego is an organized entity, whereas the id is not; in fact, the ego is the organized part of the id. It would be quite unjustifiable to conceive of the ego and the id as if they were two opposing camps—as though through repression the ego were seeking to suppress a part of the id, and that thereupon the rest of the id came to the assistance of the part attacked and measured its strength against that of the ego. Such may often come about, but it is certainly not the situation at the outset, at the time when repression is instituted; as a rule, the instinctual impulse to be repressed remains isolated. The act of repression has demonstrated to us the strength of the ego, but it also bears witness at the same time to the ego's impotence and to the uninfluenceable character of the individual instinctual impulse in the id. For the process which through repression has become a symptom now maintains its existence outside of the ego-organization and independent of it. And not it alone, but all its offshoots, enjoy the same privilege of extraterritoriality, as one might put it; and where these come into associative contact with parts of the ego-organization, it becomes a question whether they will not win the latter over to their side and batten on this success at the expense of the ego. A thrice-familiar comparison depicts the symptom as a foreign body which produces and maintains uninterruptedly symptoms of stimulus and response in the tissues in which it has become embedded. It may happen, it is true, that the defensive struggle against the unwelcome instinctual impulse is terminated when a symptom is formed; as far as we know, this is most likely to occur in hysterical conversion, but as a rule the course of events is otherwise; after the first act of repression there follows a lengthy or never-ending epilogue: the struggle against the instinctual impulse is continued in the struggle against the symptom.

This secondary defensive struggle presents two mutually contradictory aspects. On the one hand, the ego is compelled by its nature to undertake something which we must regard as an attempt at reinstatement or propitiation. The ego is an organization; it is dependent on the free intercommunication of, and the possibility of reciprocal interplay between, all its constituent elements; its desexualized energy still gives evidence of its origin in its striving for union and unification, and this compulsion to synthesis increases in direct proportion to the strength which the ego attains. It can thus be understood that the ego also attempts to do away with the alien and isolated character of the symptom by utilizing every possibility of binding it to itself in some way and of incorporating it within its organization by means of such ties. We know that an effort of this kind is already at work in the creating of the symptom. A classical example of this is afforded by those hysterical symptoms which so transparently constitute a compromise between the wish for gratification and the need for punishment. As representing the fulfillment of a demand on the part of the superego such symptoms are *ab initio* an integral part of the ego, while on the other hand they signify loci of the repressed material and points where the latter has broken into the ego-organization; they are, so to speak, frontier posts staffed from both sides of the border. The question whether all primary hysterical symptoms are so constructed should merit careful investigation. In the further course of events the ego behaves as if it were swayed by the consideration that the symptom is there and cannot be got rid of, and that therefore the thing to do is to make the best of the situation and extract the greatest advantage possible from it. There takes place an adaptation to the ego-alien bit of the world within, which the

symptom represents—an adaptation such as otherwise the ego would normally effect to the outer
world of reality. Occasions for so doing are never
lacking. The existence of the symptom may entail
a certain impairment of the efficiency with which
a demand on the part of the superego may be
silenced or a claim on the part of the environment
repudiated. Thus the symptom is gradually en-
trusted with the representing of important inter-
ests; it acquires a value for self-assertion; it becomes
intertwined more and more intimately with the
ego, becoming ever more indispensable to the latter. Only in rather rare instances does the encapsul-
ation of a foreign body reproduce anything similar
to this. One would exaggerate the significance of
this secondary adaptation if one were to say that
the ego acquired the symptom for the sole purpose
of enjoying its advantages. This would be to advance a view as correct or as erroneous as the opinion that a maimed war veteran had had his leg shot
away only that he might thereafter live in indolence
on his pension.

Other symptom complexes, those of compulsion
neurosis and paranoia, acquire high value for the
ego, not because they bring it some advantage, but
because they yield a narcissistic gratification other-

wise denied. The systems formed by the compulsion neurotic flatter his self-love with the illusion that because of his particular cleanliness and conscientiousness he is better than other people; the delusions of paranoia open up to the ingenuity and the fantasy of these patients a field of activity not easily replaced. From all these interrelationships there results what we know as the (secondary) *gain of illness* of neurosis. This comes to the aid of the ego in its effort to incorporate the symptom within itself, and strengthens the fixation of the latter. When, then, we attempt to render analytic assistance to the ego in its struggle against the symptom, we find these reconciling bonds between the ego and the symptom functioning on the side of the resistances. To loosen them is not made easy for us. The two devices which the ego employs against the symptom really stand in opposition to each other.

The other of the two devices has a less friendly character; it continues the original trend of repression. But it seems that we need not bring a charge of inconsistency against the ego. The ego is peace-loving and would like to incorporate the symptom, to include it in its ensemble. The disturbance proceeds from the symptom, which, as the true substitute for and derivative of the repressed striving, continues to play the rôle of the latter, unceasingly reiterates its demand for gratification, and thus compels the ego to give the signal of distress and to put itself on guard.

The secondary struggle of defense against the symptom is protean in its character, is enacted in various arenas, and makes use of a multiplicity of means. We shall not be able to say very much about it, however, unless we take individual instances of symptom creation as the subject of discussion. In doing so we shall find occasion to embark upon the problem of anxiety which for some time now we have felt to be lurking in the background. It will be desirable to begin with the symptoms which hysteria creates; we are not yet prepared for hypotheses concerning the process of symptom formation in compulsion neurosis, paranoia and other neuroses.

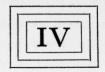

Infantile Zoöphobia

THE first case which we shall consider is that of
an infantile hysterical zoöphobia, taking as
an example a case, typical in all essential respects,
of a phobia of horses, the case of "little Hans." [1]
The very first impression we derive makes it evident that the conditions which obtain in an actual
case of neurotic illness are far more complicated
than we should be led to expect as long as we work
with abstractions only. It is something of a task to
get one's bearings with regard to what the repressed
impulse is and what its substitute in the form of
symptoms, and wherein the motive for repression
becomes recognizable.

Little Hans refused to go out on the street because he was afraid of horses. This is the raw material of the case. Now, what is it in this which is
the symptom: the development of anxiety, or the
choice of the object of anxiety, or the renouncing

[1] See *The Analysis of a Phobia in a Five-Year-Old Boy*, Collected Papers, Vol. III.

of freedom of movement, or several of these com-
bined? What is the gratification which he renounces? Why does he have to renounce it?

It would be easy enough to reply that there is
nothing so very puzzling about this case. The un-
intelligible fear of horses is the symptom; the in-
ability to go out on the street is an inhibition, a
restriction, which the ego imposes on itself in order
not to arouse anxiety. The correctness of the explanation of this last point is sufficiently evident, and
this inhibition may therefore be left out of account
in our subsequent discussion. But this cursory
initial acquaintance with the case does not even
give us the true text of the manner in which the
alleged symptom is expressed. For, as we learn on
closer inquiry, it is not at all a question of an
indefinite fear of horses, but of a definite anxious
expectation—namely, that of being bitten by a
horse. This content, it is true, seeks to avoid becoming conscious and to be replaced by the indefinite phobia in which only the anxiety and
its object still remain. Is this content perhaps the
nucleus of the symptom?

We shall make no further progress so long as we
fail to take into account the entire psychic situation
of the little patient as this is revealed to us during

analysis. He finds himself in the jealous and hostile œdipus attitude to his father, whom, however, in so far as his mother does not enter into the picture as the cause of dissension, he loves devotedly. Thus we have a conflict springing from ambivalence—a firmly founded love and a not less justified hatred, both directed to the same person. His phobia must be an attempt to resolve this conflict. Such conflicts due to ambivalence are very common; we are acquainted with another typical outcome of them in which one of the two contending trends, usually the tender one, becomes enormously augmented, while the other disappears. Only the excessiveness of the tenderness and its compulsive character betray the fact that this attitude is not the only one present, and that it is ever on its guard to keep the contrary attitude suppressed, making it possible to construe a train of events which we describe as repression through *reaction formation* (in the ego). Cases like that of little Hans show nothing of such reaction formation; evidently there are various paths of escape from an ambivalency conflict.

Meanwhile there is something else which we have perceived with certainty. The instinctual impulse which succumbs to repression is a hostile impulse against the father. The analysis furnished the evidence of this in tracing the origin of the idea of the biting horse. Hans saw a horse fall down; he saw too a playmate with whom he had played "horsie" fall and hurt himself. The analytic material has given us the right to construe a wish on Hans's part to the effect that his father should fall and hurt himself as had the horse and Hans's playmate. References of his to a departure which he saw his father make lead us to suppose that the wish for his father's destruction has also found less timid expression. Such a wish, however, is equivalent to the intention of doing away with him himself, to the murderous impulse of the œdipus complex.

From this repressed instinctual impulse there exists as yet no pathway to the substitute for it which we assume the phobia of horses to be. Let us now simplify little Hans's emotional situation by leaving out the infantile factor and the ambivalence; let us call him a younger servant in a household who is in love with the mistress of the house and enjoys certain favors at her hands. We will retain too the element that he hates the master of the house, who is of course stronger than he, and wishes he had some means of getting him out of the way; the most natural upshot of this situation then is that he would fear revenge or retaliation on the

part of this master, that a state of anxiety in relation to him would be engendered—quite like little
Hans's phobia of horses. But this means that we
cannot term his phobic anxiety a symptom; if little
Hans, in love with his mother, were to betray fear
of his father, we should have no right to ascribe a
neurosis, a phobia, to him. We should, rather, be
confronted merely with a wholly intelligible affective reaction. That which makes this affective reaction into a neurosis is singly and solely an altogether different feature, namely, the substituting
of the horse for the father. It is this displacement,
therefore, which produces something deserving of
the term symptom; and this is that other mechanism we have spoken of which permits the resolving
of the ambivalency conflict without recourse to
reaction formation. This displacement, moreover,
is rendered possible or facilitated by the circum-
stance that inborn traces of a totemistic mode of
thinking can still be easily activated at this tender
age; the gulf between man and animal is not yet
recognized, certainly not so overemphasized as
later. The adult male, admired but also feared,
still belongs in the same category with large animals, which one envies for many things but against
which one has also been warned because they can

be dangerous. Thus the conflict due to ambivalence is not worked out in the same person, but is, so to speak, detoured, in that one of its component impulses is foisted upon another person as substitute.

Thus far matters are clear enough, but on another score the analysis of little Hans's phobia has been highly disappointing. The distortion of which the symptom consists is carried out not at all upon the representative (the ideational content) of the instinctual impulse to be repressed, but upon an entirely different one which corresponds only to a reaction against what is unwelcome *per se*. Our expectation would rather have been that little Hans would have developed, instead of his fear of horses, a tendency to maltreat them, to beat them, or would have given clear expression to his wish to see them fall down and injure themselves, possibly to die in convulsions (the "making a row with the feet" [1]). Something of the kind really occurred during his analysis, but it is not at all conspicuous in his neurosis, and—curiously enough—if he had developed such hostility as a central symptom, directed against horses only instead of against his father, we should certainly not have judged that he had a neurosis. There is something wrong here somewhere, either

[1] *Loc. cit.*, page 193.—TRANSLATOR'S NOTE.

in our conception of repression or in our definition of a symptom. One thing of course strikes us immediately: If little Hans had really manifested such an attitude towards horses, then repression would not have altered in the least the character of the objectionable aggressive instinctual impulse but only transformed its object.

It is quite certain that there are cases of repression which do not do more than this. In the genesis of little Hans's phobia, however, more has happened; how much more, we may discover from another analytic fragment.

We already know that little Hans gave as the content of his phobia the idea of being bitten by a horse. Now we have since obtained insight into the genesis of another case of zoöphobia wherein it was a wolf which gave rise to anxiety but which likewise represented a father substitute.[1] In connection with a dream which the analysis was able to elucidate, this boy developed a fear of being eaten by a wolf, like one of the seven little goats in the fairy story. The authenticated fact that little Hans's father had played "horsie" with him was certainly a determining factor in his choice of the animal causing anx-

---

[1] See *From the History of an Infantile Neurosis*, Collected Papers, Vol. III.

iety; in the same way, it is at least highly probable that the father of this second patient, a Russian analyzed in his twenties, had mimicked a wolf in playing with him as a youngster and had jokingly threatened to eat him up. I have since come upon a third case, that of a young American, who did not develop any animal phobia, it is true, yet in whom its very absence helped to an understanding of the other cases. His sexual excitement had been kindled by a fantastic nursery tale which was read to him of an Arab sheik who pursued a Gingerbread Man in order to devour him. With this edible being he identified himself, the sheik was readily recognizable as a father substitute, and this fantasy became the first substratum of his autoerotic activity. The idea of being eaten by the father belongs to the typical primal stock of childhood ideas; analogies from mythology (Kronos) and from animal life are generally familiar.

Despite such assistance, these ideas are so foreign to us that it is only with incredulity that we are able to concede them to the child. We also do not know whether they really mean what they seem to express, and do not understand how they can become the subject of a phobia. Analytic experience, of course, gives us the required information. It tells us that the idea of being eaten by the father is the regressively debased expression of a tender passive impulse which craves to be the object of the father's love in the sense of genital erotism. The further history of the case permits of no doubt as to the correctness of this interpretation. The genital impulse, it is true, no longer betrays anything of its tender intent when it is expressed in the language of the stage of transition from the oral to the sadistic phase of libido organization, a stage long since left behind. Is it, moreover, a question only of a substitution of the instinct representative by a regressive mode of expression, or is it, rather, a genuine regressive debasement of the genitally directed impulse in the id? This seems to be a matter by no means easy to decide. The clinical history of the Russian "wolf man" points quite definitely to the latter more serious possibility, for from the time of the crucial dream forward he behaved "naughtily," cruelly and sadistically, and developed shortly afterwards an outright compulsion neurosis. At all events we learn that repression is not the only means at the command of the ego whereby it defends itself against an unwelcome instinctual drive. When it succeeds in bringing about the regression of the impulse, it has inflicted more radical damage upon the latter, after all, than would be possible through repression. Occasionally, to be sure, repression follows upon the regression which the ego has first compelled.

The situation in the case of the "wolf man" and the somewhat simpler one in that of little Hans suggest a number of further considerations, but two unexpected pieces of insight we obtain at once. There can be no doubt that the repressed instinctual impulse which these phobias represent is a hostile one directed against the father. One may say that this impulse is repressed by a process of transformation into its opposite; in place of aggression against the father, there appears the father's aggression—retaliation—against the individual himself. Since such aggression is rooted in the sadistic stage of libido development in any case, there is only necessary a certain degree of degradation thereof to the oral level, such as is intimated in the case of Hans in the being bitten, but in the Russian is carried out in more forthright fashion in the being eaten. But in addition analysis makes it possible to establish beyond any doubt that simultaneously still another instinctual impulse has succumbed to repression, one of opposite signification, namely, a tender passive impulse towards the father which had already reached the threshold of the genital (phallic) stage of libido organization. This latter seems even to be the more significant as regards the end-result of the repressive process; it undergoes the more extensive regression; it obtains the decisive influence upon the content of the phobia. Where therefore we have traced the repression of but a single impulse, we have now to recognize the conjunction of two such processes; the two instinctual impulses concerned—sadistic aggression against the father, and a tender passive attitude to him—form a contrasting pair; nay, more: if we evaluate the history of little Hans correctly, we recognize that in addition the tender object-cathexis of his mother has been abolished through the creation of his phobia, although of this the content of the phobia betrays no suggestion. We are dealing in the case of Hans—it is much less definite in the case of the Russian—with a repression which involves almost every component of the œdipus complex— the hostile as well as the tender impulse towards the father, and the tender towards the mother.

These are quite unwelcome complications for us whose desire it was to study only simple cases of symptom formation resulting from repression, and who had turned for this purpose to the simplest and seemingly most transparent neuroses, those of childhood. Instead of a single repression we encountered a host of them, and in addition to this we had to deal with regression as well. Perhaps we have only increased the confusion by attempting to fit both our analyses of zoöphobia, of little Hans and of the "wolf man," into the same Procrustean bed. For certain differences between the two now strike us. It is only of little Hans that we may declare with assurance that through his phobia he overcomes the two major impulses of the œdipus complex, the aggressive impulse towards the father and the over-tender impulse towards the mother; tender feelings towards his father are certainly present also and play their part in the repression of their opposite, but it cannot be shown either that they were strong enough to provoke repression or that they were abolished subsequently. Hans seems to have been quite a normal youngster, with a so-called positive œdipus complex. It is possible that the elements which we fail to find were also co-active in him, but we cannot demonstrate them; the material even of our most thorough analyses is simply deficient, our documentation incomplete. In the case of the Russian the lacuna occurs at another point; his relation to the female object was disturbed by a premature seduction, the passive feminine component was strongly developed in him, and the analysis of his wolf dream reveals little of intended aggression against his father—all these provide the most unequivocal proof that the repression has to do with the passive tender attitude to the father. Here again it may be that other factors played a part, but they are not in evidence. If, despite these differences between the two cases, which are almost of the nature of a complete antithesis, the end-result of the phobia is nearly the same, the explanation of this fact must come from another source; it comes from the second result of our little comparative study. We believe that we know the motive force behind the repression in both cases and see its rôle substantiated by the course which the development of the two children takes. This motive force is in both cases the same— namely, fear of a threatened castration. It is because of castration anxiety that little Hans renounces aggression against his father; his anxiety lest a horse should bite him can be readily supplemented by saying that his anxiety is lest a horse should bite off his genital, castrate him. But it is from castration anxiety also that the little Russian renounces the wish to be loved by his father as a sexual object,

for he has understood that such a relationship
would have as its prerequisite that he sacrifice his
genital—that which distinguishes him from the female. Both forms of the œdipus complex—the normal, active, as well as the inverted—founder on the
castration complex. The Russian's fear of being
eaten by a wolf contains no suggestion of castration,
it is true; through oral regression the idea has been
removed too far from the phallic stage; but the
analysis of his dream makes any other proof superfluous. It is furthermore a complete triumph of
repression that in the wording of the phobia there
is no longer anything which hints at castration.

It is in this, then, that our unexpected result consists: In both cases the motor force behind the repression is castration anxiety; and the content of
the anxiety—being bitten by a horse, or eaten by a
wolf—is in each case a distortion of and substitute
for another content, that of being castrated by the
father. It is precisely this content which has undergone repression as such. In the Russian the content
was the expression of a wish which could not maintain itself against the revolt of masculinity; in Hans
the expression of a reaction which converted aggression into its opposite. But the anxiety affect of
the phobia which constitutes its essence does not

arise from the process of repression nor out of the libidinal cathexes of the repressed impulses, but from the repressing forces themselves; the anxiety of zoöphobia is transformed castration anxiety, therefore a real anxiety, a reality fear, fear of a danger actually threatening or believed to do so. Here it is the anxiety that causes the repression, and not, as I earlier stated, the repression the anxiety.

It is not pleasant to think of it, but there is no use in denying that I have repeatedly put forward the thesis that through repression the instinctual representative is distorted, displaced, and the like, and the libido of the instinctual impulse transformed into anxiety. Study of the phobias, which should be particularly well calculated to furnish proof of this thesis, thus fails to confirm it; rather, it seems completely to contradict it. The fear in zoöphobia is castration anxiety on the part of the ego, that in agoraphobia (though this has been less thoroughly studied) seems to be a fear of temptation, which must certainly be related genetically to castration anxiety. The majority of phobias, so far as we can see at present, are traceable to such a fear on the ego's part of the demands of the libido. Always in this situation it is the attitude of anxiety on the part of the ego which is the motive of and

the incitement to repression. Never does the anxiety emanate from the repressed libido. If I had
been content on earlier occasions simply to say that
following upon repression a certain amount of anxiety appears in place of the expression of libido
that would be expected, I should not have to re-
tract anything now. The description is correct, and
there does exist the correspondence between the
strength of the impulse to be repressed and the
intensity of the anxiety resulting which I asserted.
But I confess I thought I was giving more than a
mere description; I supposed that I had recognized
the metapsychological process of a direct transformation of libido into anxiety; this I can no longer
maintain today. I was unable, besides, to give any
account at that earlier time of how such a transformation was accomplished.

Whence did I derive at all the idea of this transformation? At a time when we were still a long way
from distinguishing between processes in the ego
and processes in the id, from a study of the "actual"
neuroses. I found that certain sexual practices, such
as coitus interruptus, frustrated excitement, en-
forced abstinence, give rise to outbreaks of anxiety
and a general predisposition to anxiety—which may
be induced whenever, therefore, sexual excitation

is inhibited, frustrated or diverted in the course of its discharge in gratification. Since sexual excitement is the expression of libidinal instinctual impulses, it did not seem rash to suppose that through the influence of such disturbances the libido became converted into anxiety. Now this observation still holds good today; on the other hand, it cannot be denied that the libido of processes in the id is subjected to disturbance by the provocative influence of repression; thus it may still be correct to say that in repression anxiety is created out of the libidinal cathexis of instinctual impulses. But how is one to bring this finding into accord with the other, namely, that the anxiety of a phobia is an ego anxiety, originates in the ego, and does not result from repression but on the contrary evokes it? This seems a contradiction, and one not simple to resolve. To reduce the two sources of anxiety to a single one is not easy of accomplishment. One may attempt it by supposing that in the situation of interrupted coitus, of intermittent excitation, of abstinence, the ego scents danger to which it reacts with anxiety; but this does not get us very far forward. On the other hand, the analysis of phobias which we have undertaken does not seem to be open to correction. *Non liquet!*

Symptom Formation and the
Secondary Defense of the Ego

I T WAS our desire to study the way in which symptoms are created, and the secondary struggle of the ego against them, but in selecting phobias for this purpose we have evidently not made a very fortunate choice. Anxiety, which is the predominating characteristic of these disorders, now appears as a complication which conceals the true state of affairs. There is a plenitude of neuroses in which no anxiety is manifested. True conversion hysteria belongs in this category; its most severe symptoms may be free from any admixture of anxiety. This fact alone ought to serve as a warning to us not to connect anxiety with symptom formation too rigidly. The phobias are in other respects so closely related to conversion hysteria that I have considered it justifiable to align the former with the latter as "anxiety hysteria." But no one has yet been able to formulate what it really is that determines whether

a case will assume the form of a conversion hysteria
or of a phobia; in other words, no one has established what constitutes the prerequisite for the development of anxiety in hysteria.

The symptoms most frequent in conversion hysteria—motor paralyses, contractures, or involuntary movements or motor discharge; pain; hallucinations—are cathectic processes either permanently
sustained or intermittent; but to say this only introduces new difficulties into their explanation.
One really does not know much that can be said
about these symptoms. Through analysis one may
learn for what particular excitation whose discharge is interfered with they are the substitute;
in most instances we find that the symptoms themselves participate in this discharge of excitation, as
if the total energy of the excitation had been concentrated upon this one fraction. Pain was present
in the situation in which repression took place;
hallucinations were the perception of, motor paralysis the defense against, an action which should
have been carried out in that situation but was
inhibited; contracture is usually a displacement
elsewhere of a muscle innervation intended at the
time in question; the convulsive seizure the expression of an outbreak of affect which has escaped

from the normal control of the ego. The sensation of unpleasure (*Unlust*) which accompanies the appearance of symptoms varies to an extraordinary degree. In the case of the permanent symptoms where a displacement upon motility has occurred, such as paralyses and contractures, it is usually absent; the ego behaves towards them as if it were not involved; in the case of the intermittent symptoms and those in the sensory sphere, definite feelings of unpleasure are experienced as a rule, which may be increased to an excessive degree in the case of the symptom of pain. It is extremely difficult to isolate out of this complexity the factor which makes such differences possible and which would permit of their explanation on a single all-inclusive basis. Furthermore, there is little to note in conversion hysteria regarding the struggle of the ego against the symptom, once the latter has been created. It is only when the sensibility to pain on the part of some portion of the body has become a symptom that the part of the body in question is placed in the position of playing a double rôle. The painful symptom makes its appearance just as certainly if this part of the body is stimulated from without as when the pathogenic situation which the symptom represents is associatively activated from within, and the ego adopts precautionary measures to forestall the activation of the symptom through external perception. What the cause is of the particular obscurity which surrounds symptom formation in conversion hysteria we are unable to guess, but it supplies a reason for quickly leaving this unfruitful field behind.

We turn to the compulsion neurosis in the expectation that we may learn more in this disorder of the way in which symptoms are created. The symptoms of compulsion neurosis are, broadly speaking, of two kinds and of contradictory purport. Either they are prohibitions or prophylactic measures or atonements, and are thus of a negative character, or they are on the other hand substitute gratifications, very often in symbolic guise. Of these two groups the negative, defensive, punitive variety is the earlier; with the progress of the illness, however, the gratifications, proof against all measures of defense, gain the upper hand. It represents a triumph of symptom creation when this process succeeds in amalgamating prohibition with gratification, so that the originally defensive command or prohibition acquires the significance of a gratification, for which purpose highly artificial associative links are often utilized. In this performance is manifest that tendency to synthesis which we have already attributed to the ego. In extreme cases the patient succeeds in bringing it about that the majority of his symptoms acquire a meaning the exact opposite of that which they originally possessed—a testimonial to the power of that ambivalence which plays so large a rôle, though we do not know why, in compulsion neurosis. In the extremest case the symptom is dichronous; that is to say, upon a piece of behavior which carries out a given prescription there follows immediately a second one which abolishes or nullifies it, even though not yet venturing to institute its opposite.

Two impressions emerge immediately from this cursory survey of compulsive symptoms. The first is that in these symptoms a continuous struggle against the repressed is being maintained, in which the tide of battle turns increasingly against the repressing forces; the second, that ego and super-ego here participate to a particularly large degree in the formation of symptoms.

Compulsion neurosis is indeed the most interesting and most grateful subject of analytic investigation, but a problem still unsolved. If we wish to penetrate more deeply into its nature, we shall have to confess that dubious assumptions and unproven conjectures cannot yet be dispensed with. The situation of origin in the case of compulsion neurosis is in fact none other than that in hysteria, namely, the defense necessary against the libidinal demands of the œdipus complex. Furthermore there seems to be present in every compulsion neurosis a lowermost layer of hysterical symptoms of very early formation. Its subsequent form, however, is then decisively altered by a constitutional factor. The genital organization of the libido proves to be too feeble and too little resistant. When the ego undertakes the measures of defense just referred to, the first result it achieves is that the genital organization (of the phallic phase) is wholly or partially thrown back to the earlier anal-sadistic stage. This fact of regression is crucial for all that follows.

One may take still another possibility into consideration. Perhaps the regression is not the consequence of a constitutional but of a time factor. It is made possible, not because the genital organization of the libido has proved too feeble, but because the resistance of the ego has been initiated too early, during the height of the sadistic phase. I do not venture a definite decision on this point, but analytic observation does not favor the latter supposition. It indicates, rather, that the phallic stage has already been reached when the deviation to compulsion neurosis occurs. The age period, furthermore, at which this neurosis has its onset is a later one than is the case with hysteria (the second period of childhood, after the latency period); in one case which I had the opportunity to study, in which this disorder developed very late, it was clear that a disturbance in actual life of the patient's genitality, which had been intact until then, supplied the situation prerequisite for regression and for the genesis of the compulsion neurosis.[1]

The metapsychological explanation of regression I have thought to find in an "instinct defusion," in the segregation of the erotic components which with the onset of the genital phase were joined to the destructive cathexes of the sadistic stage.

The enforcing of regression constitutes the ego's first success in its struggle of defense against the demands of the libido. It is convenient to distinguish here the general tendency to "defense" from "repression," which is only one of the mecha-

---

[1] See *The Predisposition to Obsessional Neurosis*, Collected Papers, Vol. II.

nisms utilized in the service of defense. Perhaps in compulsion neurosis, even more clearly than in normal and hysterical cases, we may recognize the castration complex as the motivating force of defense, the strivings of the œdipus complex as that which is defended against. We now find ourselves at the beginning of the latency period, which is characterized by the breaking down of the œdipus complex, the creating or consolidating of the superego, and the erecting of ethical and æsthetic barriers in the ego. In compulsion neurosis these phenomena exceed the normal degree; to the destruction of the œdipus complex is joined the regressive degradation of the libido, the superego becomes particularly strict and hardhearted, and in obedience to the superego the ego develops intense reaction formations of conscientiousness, pity, cleanliness. With inexorable and hence not always successful severity the temptation to continue the masturbation of early infancy is tabooed—a temptation now based upon regressive (anal-sadistic) ideas, but at the same time representing the uncontrolled part of the phallic organization. An inner contradiction consists in the fact that it is precisely in the interest of the maintenance of masculinity (castration anxiety) that every manifestation of this masculinity is prevented, but in compulsion neurosis this contradiction also is only exaggerated, merely an intensification of the normal manner of overcoming the œdipus complex. Just as every excess carries within itself the seeds of its own surcease, so this holds true too of compulsion neurosis, in that it is precisely the suppressed onanism which in the form of compulsive acts compels an ever furthered approximation to gratification.

The reaction formations in the ego of the compulsion neurotic which we recognize as exaggerations of normal character traits we may put down as a new mechanism of defense, along with regression and repression. They seem to be lacking, or to be much weaker, in hysteria. In retrospect we thus arrive at a conjecture as to what it is that distinguishes the defense process in hysteria. It appears that this is limited to repression, in that the ego turns away from the objectionable instinctual impulse, leaves it to work out its destiny in the unconscious, and takes no further interest in its fate. This cannot be correct to the last detail, for certainly we know cases in which the hysterical symptom signifies at the same time the fulfillment of a demand for punishment on the part of the superego, but it will describe a general characteristic of the behavior of the ego in hysteria.

It may simply be taken as a fact that in compulsion neurosis so strict a superego is formed, or one may give consideration to the fact that the fundamental characteristic of this disorder is regression of the libido, and attempt to connect with this the character of the superego. As a matter of fact, the superego, which derives from the id, is quite unable to evade the regression and instinct defusion which take place there. It can hardly be surprising if the superego, on its part, should be more rigid, more sadistic, more hardhearted than in normal development.

During the latency period the defense against the temptation to onanism seems to be regarded as the principal task. This struggle gives rise to a number of symptoms which recur in typical fashion in the most various individuals and which have in general the character of a ceremonial. It is greatly to be deplored that these have not thus far been collected and systematically analyzed; as the earliest manifestations of neurosis, they would most easily throw light upon the mechanism of symptom formation here employed. They already

exhibit the characteristics which will become manifest so ominously later on in a serious illness: such
as their application to acts which should later be
carried out as if they were automatic, as, for example, going to bed, washing and dressing, and
locomotion; and such as also the tendency to repetition and to procrastination. Why this should
happen, we are as yet far from understanding; the
sublimation of anal-erotic components plays a definite rôle therein.

Puberty forms a definite epoch in the development of the compulsion neurosis. The genital organization, interrupted in childhood, is now re-
sumed with great vigor. But we know that the
sexual development of childhood also prescribes
the direction taken by this pubertal recrudescence.
Thus on the one hand the aggressive impulses of
childhood will reawaken; on the other, a greater
or smaller proportion of the fresh libidinal impulses—in severe cases, their totality—must take the
road laid down in advance by regression and appear as aggressive and destructive designs. In consequence of this disguising of the erotic strivings
and of the intense reaction formations in the ego,
the struggle against sexuality is now continued
under an ethical ægis. The ego rebels in bewilder-

ment against the cruel and outrageous demands which are sent out from the id into consciousness, little suspecting that it is combating erotic wishes in so doing—among them also such as would otherwise escape its protest. The overstrict superego insists the more actively on the suppression of sexuality since the latter has assumed such obnoxious forms. Thus in compulsion neurosis the conflict is seen to be intensified in two directions: the defending forces have become too intolerant, that against which the defense is instituted too intolerable—and both of these through the influence of the single factor of regression of the libido.

One might find a contradiction of a number of our assumptions in the fact that the unwelcome obsession is conscious at all. What is alone indubitable is that it has previously undergone repression. In general, the specific terms of the aggressive instinctual impulse are not at all known to the ego. A good deal of analytic work is necessary to bring them to consciousness. What has penetrated into consciousness is as a rule only a distorted substitute, rendered unrecognizable either by a hazy and dreamlike vagueness or through an absurd disguise. If repression has not left its impress upon the content of the aggressive impulse, it has at least done away with the affect accompanying it. Thus it is that the aggression does not appear to the ego as an impulse but rather, as patients put it, as a pure "thought content" which should leave one cold. The remarkable thing is that this is not in fact the case.

The affect not shown on perceiving the compulsive idea does make its appearance, but elsewhere. The superego behaves as if no repression had taken place, as if it were fully cognizant of the aggressive impulse in its true meaning and with its affective character undiminished; and it treats the ego on the basis of this hypothesis. The ego which knows on the one hand that it is innocent has on the other to experience a feeling of guilt and to carry a feeling of responsibility which it is unable to account for. The riddle which this presents for our solution is not so difficult, however, as at first sight it appears. The attitude of the superego is entirely intelligible; the contradiction in the ego shows us only that by the medium of repression it has shut itself off from the id while remaining wholly accessible to influence from the superego.[1] The further question why the ego does not also seek to throw off the harassing criticism

---

[1] *Cf.* Reik: *Geständniszwang und Strafbedürfnis,* 1925, page 51.

of the superego is settled by the information that this actually happens in a large number of cases. There are also cases of compulsion neurosis quite without a sense of guilt; to the best of our present understanding, the ego has saved itself from the perception of guilt by means of a new series of self-punitive symptoms, atonements, and restrictions. These symptoms signify at the same time, however, gratifications of masochistic instinctual impulses which likewise derive reënforcement from regression.

So enormous is the multiplicity of the manifestations which compulsion neuroses exhibit that despite all effort no one has yet succeeded in providing a comprehensive synthesis of all their variations. One is tempted to lay stress upon typical relationships, although in doing so there is the ever present fear of overlooking others no less important.

I have already described the general trend of symptom formation in compulsion neurosis. It consists in giving more and more room to substitute gratification at the expense of renunciation. The same symptoms which originally had the signification of limitations imposed upon the ego later assume also, thanks to the ego's synthesizing tendency, that of gratification, and it is evident enough that the latter significance gradually becomes the more potent one. An ego upon which extreme restrictions are imposed and which on this account is reduced to seeking gratification in symptoms is the result of this process, which increasingly approximates to a complete miscarriage of the original effort at defense. The shifting of the balance of power in favor of gratification may lead to the ominous end-result of a paralysis of the will on the part of the ego, which in every decision finds almost as strong an impulsion arrayed on one side of the question as on the other. The excessively bitter conflict between id and superego which dominates the disorder from the beginning may become so extended that none of the activities of the ego, incapable as it is of mediation, can escape involvement in this conflict.

The Undoing and Isolation
Mechanics in Compulsion Neurosis

D URING this struggle of the ego it is possible to
observe two symptom-producing activities on
its part which are of particular interest because
they are obvious surrogates for repression and on
this account serve admirably to illustrate the purpose and technique of the latter. Perhaps also the
fact that these adjuvant and substitutive techniques come upon the scene may be looked upon
as proof that the accomplishing of repression in
the usual sense meets with difficulties. If we bear
it in mind that in compulsion neurosis the ego is
the arena of symptom formation to a much greater
degree than in hysteria, that this ego clings tenaciously to its contact with reality and its relation
to consciousness, and to this end summons all the
intellectual means at its command—nay, more than
this, that thinking appears to be hypercathected,
erotized—if we bear these things in mind, such

variants of repression as we have just referred to will perhaps seem less strange to us.

The two techniques I allude to are those of *undoing* and *isolation*. The first of these has an extensive sphere of application and reaches back to a very early period of development. It is a kind of negative magic which by means of a motor symbolism would "blow away," as it were, not the consequences of an event (an impression, an experience), but the event itself. The choice of the expression I have used—"blow away"—is a reference to the rôle which such a technique plays, not alone in neurosis, but in magic, in folkways, and in religious ceremonial. In compulsion neurosis the mechanism of "undoing" is first and foremost encountered in the dichronous symptoms in which the individual's second act abrogates or nullifies the first, in such manner that it is as though neither had taken place, whereas in reality both have done so. Compulsive ceremonials have the intention to "undo" as their second root, their first being to prevent or to forestall some specific thing happening or being repeated. The distinction is easy enough to grasp; precautionary measures are of a rational character, "voiding" or "cancelling" by means of "undoing" of an irrational, magical nature. Naturally one must suppose that this second root is the older, that it derives from the animistic attitude to the environment. The effort at "undoing" finds its reflection in the normal sphere in the resolve to treat an occurrence as *non arrivé;* but in this case one does not take up arms against it, one is simply not concerned about either the occurrence or its consequences; whereas in neurosis the attempt is made to abrogate the past itself, to repress it by motor means. An effort of the same sort may provide the explanation of the compulsion to *repetition* so frequently present in neurosis, a repetition in the carrying out of which various mutually contradictory purposes are commingled. What has not happened in such a way as would have accorded with one's desire is made, through its repetition in some other way, not to have happened at all—to which are super-added all the various motives which may exist for lingering upon these repetitions. In the further course of the neurosis the striving to "undo" a traumatic experience is often revealed as a motive force of the first rank in the creating of symptoms. Thus we obtain an unexpected insight into a new and motor technique of defense, or, as we may here say with less inexactitude, of repression.

The second of the new techniques to be described, one peculiar to compulsion neurosis, is that of *isolation*. Its reference is likewise to the motor sphere; and it consists in the interposition, after an unpleasant experience, as also after some act of the subject's own which is of significance in the sense of his neurosis, of a refractory period in which nothing more is allowed to happen, no perception registered, and no action performed. This at first sight strange behavior soon betrays its relation to repression. We know that in hysteria it is possible for a traumatic impression to become subjected to amnesia, but that in compulsion neurosis this is not often achieved; the experience is not forgotten but it is stripped of its affect and its associative connections are suppressed or interrupted, so that it stands apart, as if isolated, and furthermore fails to be reproduced in the course of one's mental activity. The effect of this isolation is the same, then, as in repression with amnesia. The isolation phenomena of compulsion neurosis thus reproduce this technique, but intensified by motor means and with a magic intent. The very things which are kept asunder in this way are precisely those which associatively belong together; motor isolation is to furnish a guaranty of the interruption of coherence in thinking. A pretext for the employment of this method on the part of the neurosis is provided by the normal process of concentration. Impressions or problems that seem important to us should not be disturbed by simultaneous claims on our attention of other mental processes or activities. But even in normal persons concentration is utilized to keep at a distance not solely matters of indifference, things that are irrelevant, but in particular things which run inconveniently counter to the matter in hand. The things which are felt to be most irreconcilable in this regard are those which originally belonged together but which in the course of development have been split asunder, such as for example the manifestation in one's relation to God of the original ambivalence towards one's father, or the activity of the excretory organs as continuing to pervade erotic excitation. Thus the ego has normally a not inconsiderable task to perform in directing the course that thinking pursues, and we know that in the conduct of analysis we have to educate the ego to renounce for the time being this otherwise wholly legitimate function.

We have all had experience of the fact that it is particularly difficult for the compulsion neurotic to comply with the fundamental rule of analysis. Probably in consequence of the severe tension existing between his superego and his id, his ego is more vigilant, the isolations it effects more rigorous. It has too much to fend off in the course of its thinking—the intrusion of unconscious fantasies, the expression of ambivalent strivings. It cannot relax, it finds itself in a perpetual state of preparedness. This compulsion to concentration and isolation it then sustains through those magical acts of isolation which become so striking as symptoms and at the same time of so much significance practically, yet which are of course useless in themselves and partake of the character of a ritual.

In its attempt to prevent associations from occurring, to obstruct the forming of connections in thought, however, the ego is complying with one of the oldest and most fundamental commandments of the compulsion neurosis, the taboo on touching. To the question why the avoidance of touching, contact or contagion plays so large a rôle in the neurosis and is made the content of so complicated a system, the answer is that touching, physical contact, is the most immediate aim of aggressive no less than of tender object-cathexes.

Eros desires contact, for it strives for union, for the annihilation of spatial boundaries between ego and loved object. But destruction, too, which before the invention of long-range weapons could be effected only through proximity, necessarily presupposes physical contact, the use of the hands. To touch a woman has become in ordinary parlance a euphemism for her use as a sexual object. Not to touch the genital is the usual wording of the prohibition against autoerotic gratification. Since the compulsion neurosis sought to effect erotic contact in the first place, and then, subsequent to regression, the same contact disguised as aggression, nothing was taboo to it in such intense degree as this very contact, nothing was so fitted to become the keystone of a system of prohibitions. Isolation, however, is the abolishing of the possibility of touching, the means of withdrawing a thing from every contact; and when the neurotic isolates an impression or an action by means of an interval, he symbolically gives us to understand that he does not want the thought of the impression or the action in question to come into associative contact with other thoughts.

Such is the extent of our researches into symptom formation. It is scarcely worth while to sum-

marize them; they remain meager in result and
incomplete, and have contributed little, besides,
that was not already known. To take up for consideration symptom formation in disorders other
than the phobias, conversion hysteria and compulsion neurosis would be futile; too little is known
about it. But even grouping together these three
neuroses raises an extremely weighty question, and
one which can no longer be deferred. In all three
the destruction of the œdipus complex is the start-
ing point; in all three, we assume, castration anxiety is the motive force behind the struggles of
the ego. But it is only in the phobias that such
anxiety is manifested and acknowledged. What has
become of it in the other two? How, in the other
two, has the ego preserved itself from anxiety? The
problem becomes still more acute when we recall
the possibility previously mentioned that anxiety
arises, through a kind of fermentation, out of the
libidinal cathexis itself whose career has been interfered with; and, in addition, is it established
that castration anxiety is the only motive force
behind repression (or defense)? When one thinks
of the neuroses of women, one must doubt this;
for certain though it is that the castration complex is demonstrable in them, one can hardly speak

of castration anxiety in the strict sense where castration is already effected.[1]

---

1 See also *New Introductory Lectures on Psychoanalysis*, W. W. Norton & Company, Inc., page 121.—TRANSLATOR'S NOTE.

A Further Consideration of
Infantile Zoöphobia

L ET us return to the infantile zoöphobias, since
these cases we understand better than any
others. In these, we have seen, the ego must inter-
vene against a libidinal object-cathexis of the id
(that of the positive or negative œdipus complex,
namely), because of the recognition that to yield
to it would entail the danger of castration. This
we have already discussed, yet we may still take
occasion to clarify a doubt which remains over
from this first discussion. Shall we assume in the
case of little Hans (and thus in the case of the
positive œdipus complex) that it is the tender impulse towards the mother, or the aggressive towards
the father, which provokes measures of defense on
the part of the ego? Practically speaking, it would
seem to be a matter of indifference, particularly
since each of the two impulses predicates the other;
but a theoretical interest attaches to the question,

because only the tender impulse towards the mother can be deemed a purely erotic one. The aggressive impulse is essentially dependent upon the instinct of destruction, and we have always believed that in neurosis it is against the demands of the libido, not against those of other instincts, that the ego defends itself. As a matter of fact, we see that after the formation of the phobia the tender bond with the mother is as though dissolved, it is disposed of in thoroughgoing fashion through repression, while symptom formation has taken place as a substitute for the aggressive impulse. In the case of the "wolf man" the matter is simpler; the repressed impulse is really an erotic one, namely, the feminine attitude to the father, and it is around this impulse that symptom formation has taken place.

It is almost disgraceful that after so much labor we should still find difficulty in conceiving of the most fundamental matters, but it has been our resolve to simplify nothing and to conceal nothing. If we cannot see clearly, at least we see the obscurities clearly. What stands in our way is evidently due to the fact that our theory of instincts has developed unevenly. In the beginning we had followed the various organizations of the libido

from the oral through the anal-sadistic to the genital stage, and in so doing had equated the several
components of the sexual instinct with one another. Subsequently sadism appeared to us to be
the representative of another instinct, one opposed
to Eros. This new concept of the two classes of
instincts seems to disrupt the earlier formulation
of the occurrence of successive stages in the organization of the libido. A helpful way out of this
difficulty we do not have to invent; it has long
been ready to hand, and is to the effect that we
scarcely ever have to do with instinctual impulses
in pure form, but invariably with alloys of the
two instincts in which these are present in varying
proportions. The sadistic object-cathexis is entitled
as well, therefore, to be treated as a libidinal one;
the hypothesis of stages of organization of the
libido does not need to be revised; the aggressive
impulse towards the father is as much entitled to
be the object of repression as the tender impulse
towards the mother. At all events we will put to
one side for later consideration the possibility that
repression is a process which has a special relationship to the genital organization of the libido, and
that the ego seizes upon other methods of defense
when it has to defend itself against the libido at

other stages of its organization. A case like that of little Hans does not permit of any decision on this matter; here an aggressive impulse was dealt with through repression, but only after the genital stage had already been reached.

We do not want to lose sight at this point of the place that anxiety occupies. We have said that as soon as the ego has recognized the danger of castration, it gives the signal of anxiety, and through the medium of the pleasure-pain mechanism it inhibits, in a manner still obscure to us, the threatening cathectic process in the id. Simultaneously with this the formation of the phobia is accomplished. The castration anxiety is given another object and a distorted expression—namely, that of being bitten by a horse (or eaten by a wolf) instead of being castrated by the father. This substitute formation has two patent advantages: first, that it avoids the conflict due to ambivalence, for the father is an object who is at the same time loved; and secondly, that it allows the ego to prevent any further development of anxiety. For the anxiety of the phobia is a facultative anxiety: it makes its appearance only when its object is actually perceived. This is what one might expect; for it is only then that the danger situation is present.

Similarly, at the hands of a father who is absent castration need not be feared. Now one cannot do away with one's father; he comes and goes as he pleases. But if he is replaced by some animal, then it is only necessary to avoid the sight of that animal, that is, its presence, to be free from danger and anxiety. Little Hans therefore imposes a restriction upon his ego; he evolves the inhibition against going out in order not to encounter horses. It is even more convenient for the little Russian; it scarcely constitutes a renunciation on his part not to have anything more to do with a certain picture book. The naughty sister need only desist from showing him the picture in that book of the wolf that stood on its hind legs, and he could feel perfectly safe from his anxiety.

On a previous occasion I ascribed to phobias the character of a projection, since they substitute for an internal instinctual danger an external perceptual one. Such a process has the advantage that from an external danger protection may be gained through flight and the avoidance of the perception of it, whereas against a danger from within, flight is of no avail. This statement of mine is not incorrect, but superficial. For the instinctual demand is not in itself a danger, but is so only because it entails a true external danger, that of castration. So that fundamentally we have in the phobias, after all, merely the substituting of one external danger for another. The fact that in phobias the ego is able to escape anxiety through a process of avoidance or by means of an inhibition is in complete accord with the concept that this anxiety is simply an affective signal, and that with regard to the economic situation involved nothing has been altered.

The anxiety in zoöphobia is thus an affective reaction of the ego to danger, the danger which is in this case warned against being that of castration. There is no difference between this anxiety and the reality fear normally manifested by the ego in situations of danger, other than the fact that the content of the former remains unconscious and enters consciousness only in distorted form.

This same concept will prove to hold good, I believe, for the phobias of adults also, even though here the material which the neurosis elaborates is far more complex, and even though a number of other factors which go to the forming of symptoms are superadded. Fundamentally the situation is the same. The sufferer from agoraphobia imposes a restriction upon his ego in order to escape an

instinctual danger. The instinctual danger in question is the temptation to yield to his erotic desires;
and to yield to them would be to reincarnate once
again, as in childhood, the specter of the danger
of castration or of an analogous danger. As an example I may refer to the case of a young man who
became agoraphobic because he was afraid of yield-
ing to the allurements of prostitutes and of acquir-
ing syphilis as a punishment.

I am well aware that many cases have a more
complicated structure, and that many other repressed instinctual impulses may have their issue
in a phobia, but these are merely auxiliary and
have as a rule become attached subsequently to the
nuclear material of the neurosis. The symptomatol-
ogy of agoraphobia is complicated by the fact that
the ego is not content with renouncing something;
in addition to this, it takes steps to deprive the
situation of its danger. This additional measure is
usually a regression to childhood (in extreme cases,
to the uterus, to a period when one was protected
against the dangers which threaten today); the regression constitutes the condition under which the
renunciation need not be made. Thus the agoraphobic may go on the street provided that, like a
small child, he is accompanied by a person in

whom he has full confidence. A similar caution may also permit him to go out alone, provided that he does not go more than a certain distance away from home, that he does not enter localities which he does not know well and where the people do not know him. In the choice of these specifications there becomes manifest the influence of the infantile motives which govern him by means of his neurosis. Of quite unequivocal meaning, even without infantile regression of this sort, is the morbid fear of being alone, which would avoid the temptation to solitary masturbation. Infantile regression is, of course, conditional upon the individual's being chronologically no longer a child.

The phobia is produced, as a rule, subsequent to an initial attack of anxiety which was experienced under certain circumstances—on the street, on a railroad train, or on an occasion of being alone, for example. For the moment the anxiety is stilled, only to reappear on every occasion on which the conditions that assure protection cannot be met. The phobic mechanism works very well as a means of defense and exhibits a considerable measure of stability. A continuation of the defensive struggle, now directed against the symptom, frequently but not necessarily takes place.

What we have learned about anxiety in the phobias is applicable also to compulsion neurosis. It is not difficult to reduce the situation of the compulsion neurosis to that of the phobia. The motive force behind all later symptom formation is here clearly the ego's fear of its superego. The hostility of the superego is the danger situation which the ego must avoid. Here any semblance of projection is lacking; the danger is wholly internalized. But when we ask what it is that the ego fears at the hands of the superego, the conclusion is forced upon us that the punishment meted out by the superego is an extension of the punishment of castration. Just as the superego is the father become impersonalized, so the dread of the castration which he threatened has become converted into indefinite social anxiety or dread of conscience. But this anxiety is insured against; the ego escapes it by carrying out obediently the commands, the preventive measures and the penances imposed upon it. If it is impeded in doing this, there immediately ensues an extremely distressing sense of discomfort in which we may perceive the equivalent of anxiety and which the patient himself equates with anxiety. What we have arrived at is therefore the following: Anxiety is the reaction to a situation of danger; and it is circumvented by the ego's doing something to avoid the situation or retreat from it. One might say, then, that symptoms are created in order to avoid the development of anxiety, but such a formulation does not go below the surface. It is more accurate to say that symptoms are created in order to avoid the *danger situation* of which anxiety sounds the alarm. In the cases so far considered this danger was castration or a derivative of it.

If anxiety is the reaction of the ego to danger, then it would be the obvious thing to regard the traumatic neuroses, which are so often the sequel to exposure to danger to life, as the direct result of life- or death-anxiety, with the exclusion of any dependence, in its ætiology, upon the ego and castration. This is what was done by the majority of observers in the case of the traumatic neuroses of the last war, and it has been triumphantly claimed that proof is now at hand that jeopardy to the instinct of self-preservation is capable of giving rise to a neurosis without the participation of sexuality at all, and without regard to the complicated hypotheses of psychoanalysis. It is, as a matter of fact, extremely to be regretted that not a single reliable analysis of a case of traumatic

neurosis exists. It is to be regretted, not on account
of the objection against the ætiological significance
of sexuality, for this objection has long since been
met through the introduction of the concept of
narcissism, which brings the libidinal cathexis of
the ego into line with object-cathexes and emphasizes the libidinal nature of the instinct of self-
preservation—it is to be regretted not on this account, but rather because through the lack of such
analyses we have missed the most precious opportunity to obtain information of crucial importance
regarding the relationship between anxiety and
symptom formation. According to all that we know
of the structure of the simpler neuroses of everyday
life, it is very improbable that a neurosis should
come about only by reason of the objective fact of
exposure to danger without the participation of
the deeper unconscious strata of the mental apparatus. In the unconscious, however, there is
nothing to give content to our conception of the
destruction of life. Castration becomes, as it were,
imaginable through the daily experience of part-
ing with the contents of the bowel and through
the loss of the mother's breast which is experienced
in weaning; but nothing similar to death has ever
been experienced, or if it has been, it has left, like

fainting, no demonstrable trace. I therefore maintain that the fear of death is to be regarded as an analogue of the fear of castration, and that the situation to which the ego reacts is the state of being forsaken or deserted by the protecting super-ego—by the powers of destiny—which puts an end to security against every danger. It is also to be taken into account that in the experiences which result in traumatic neurosis the external protective mechanism against stimuli of excessive strength is broken down and excessive quanta of excitation gain access to the mental apparatus, so that here the second possibility exists that anxiety is not only employed as an affective signal but is also newly created in response to the economic demands of the situation.

With the above formulation—namely, that through regularly repeated losses of objects the ego has been prepared for castration—we have arrived at a new conception of anxiety. If we have thus far considered it as an affective signal of danger, it now appears to us, since it is so frequently a matter of the danger of castration, as the reaction to a loss, to a separation. Though various considerations which immediately occur to one seem also to tell against this conclusion, we must nevertheless be struck by a phenomenon which is in very remarkable agreement with it. The first anxiety experience, of the human being at least, is birth; and this means, objectively, separation from the mother, and could be likened to a castration of the mother (in accordance with the equation: child $=$ penis). Now it would be very satisfactory if anxiety as the symbol of a separation were to be repeated on the occasion of every subsequent separation, but unfortunately the applicability of the agreement I have just spoken of is discounted by the fact that, subjectively, birth is not at all experienced as a separation from the mother, since the mother, in the rôle of object, is entirely unknown to the completely narcissistic fœtus. Another consideration that would apply is that affective reactions to a separation are known to us, and that we experience them as grief and mourning, not as anxiety. We recall, to be sure, that in our discussion of mourning we were also unable to understand why mourning is so painful.

An Analysis of Anxiety

I T is time to take stock. What we are seeking, it is apparent, is an insight which shall reveal the nature of anxiety, an "either—or" which shall distinguish truth from error in regard to it. But this is difficult of attainment; anxiety is not a simple thing to grasp. Thus far we have arrived at nothing but contradictions, from among which no unbiased choice was possible. I now propose to order it otherwise; we will bring together in unprejudiced manner everything that can be said about anxiety, while renouncing at the same time the expectation of achieving an immediate synthesis of the problem.

Anxiety, then, is in the first place something felt. We call it an affective state, although we are equally ignorant of what an affect is. As a feeling it is of most obviously unpleasurable character, but this is not by any means a complete description of its quality; not every state of unpleasure (*Unlust*)

may we call anxiety. There are other feelings of
unpleasurable character (mental tension, sorrow,
grief), and anxiety must have other characteristics
besides this quality of unpleasure. Shall we ever
succeed, one cannot help asking, in understanding
the differences between these various affects of unpleasure?

Of the feeling of anxiety we can after all learn
something. Its character of unpleasure seems to
possess a particular note of its own—a thing difficult
to demonstrate but none the less probable, nor
would it be at all surprising if it were so. But in
addition to this special characteristic so difficult to
define, we perceive more definite physical sensations, which we refer to specific organs, as accompanying anxiety. Since the physiology of anxiety
does not interest us here, it will suffice to draw attention to specific examples of these sensations, such
as those referable to the respiratory organs and the
heart, which are the most common and the most
definite of them. They are evidence that motor
innervations, efferent processes, take part in the
total phenomenon of anxiety. The analysis of the
anxiety state gives us, then, as its attributes: (1) a
specific unpleasurable quality, (2) efferent or discharge phenomena, and (3) the perception of these.

The second and third of the foregoing supply
in themselves a distinction from similar affective
states, such as for example grief and sorrow, for
of these latter, motor manifestations do not form
an integral part; when such are present, they are
definitely distinguishable as not constituting essential constituents of the total phenomenon but consequences of or reactions to the emotional state in
question. Anxiety, therefore, is a specific state of
unpleasure accompanied by motor discharge along
definite pathways. In accordance with our general
outlook, we shall believe that an increase of excitation underlies anxiety, an increase which on the
one hand is responsible for its unpleasurable character and on the other is relieved through the discharge referred to. This purely physiological sum-
mary will scarcely satisfy us, however; we are
tempted to presume that there is an historical element present which binds the afferent and the efferent components of anxiety firmly together; in
other words, that the anxiety state is the reproduction of an experience which contains within itself
the requisite conditions for the increase in stimulation just mentioned, and for its discharge via given
pathways; and it is in virtue of this, therefore, that
the unpleasure element in anxiety acquires its

specific character. As the prototypic experience of such a sort, we think in the case of the human being of birth, and on this account we are inclined to see in the anxiety state a reproduction of the trauma of birth.

In doing so we have claimed nothing which would assign to anxiety an exceptional position among affective states. For we hold that other affects as well are reproductions of past experiences of a character vital to the organism, experiences possibly even antedating the individual; and we draw a comparison between these, as universal, specific, congenital hysterical attacks, and the seizures of the hysterical neurosis, later and individually acquired, the genesis and significance of which as memory symbols have been made clearly manifest by analysis. It would of course be most desirable to be able to demonstrate the validity of this conception for a number of other affects, but at the present time we are far from being in a position to do this.

The tracing back of anxiety to the birth experience needs justification in the face of certain obvious objections. Anxiety is a reaction characteristic of probably all organisms, certainly of all the higher ones, but birth is experienced only by mammals, and it is open to question whether for all of these birth has a traumatic significance. There is, therefore, such a thing as anxiety without a prototype in birth. But this objection takes us from psychology into biology. Precisely because anxiety, as a reaction to situations of danger, has a biologically indispensable function to fulfill it may have been contrived in different organisms in different ways. We do not know, moreover, whether in creatures at a further remove from man anxiety has the same content, afferently and efferently, as in the human being. All this does not prevent it from being the case, therefore, that anxiety, in the human being, takes the birth process as its prototype.

If this is the structure and origin of anxiety, the question then arises: What is its function? On what occasions is it reproduced? The answer seems obvious and inescapable. Anxiety arose as a response to a situation of *danger;* it will be regularly reproduced thenceforward whenever such a situation recurs.

But there is more than this to be said. The motor impulses accompanying the original anxiety state had probably as much meaning and utility as the muscular movements of the initial hysterical attack. If one would explain the hysterical seizure, one needs only, indeed, to look for the situation in which the movements in question were part of the behavior appropriate to that situation. Thus, during birth, it is probable that the directing of nerve impulses to the organs of respiration has made preparation in advance for the functioning of the lungs, the acceleration of the heart beat tended to counteract the accumulation of toxic substances in the blood. This teleology of function is of course absent from the subsequent reproduction of the anxiety state as affect, just as it is also lacking in the recurrent hysterical seizure. If therefore the individual encounters a danger situation new to him, his responding with the anxiety that constitutes the reaction to an earlier danger, instead of with the reaction appropriate to the present one, may easily become inexpedient. The suitability of the reaction reappears, however, if the danger is perceived as imminent and forewarning of it given through the outbreak of anxiety. The anxiety can then be immediately replaced by more appropriate measures for dealing with the danger. Two possibilities with regard to the appearance of anxiety, therefore, may at once be distinguished: the one, inappropriate and inexpedient, in response to a new situation of danger; the other, a useful one, as a means of giving warning of and averting such a situation.

But what is a "danger"? In the act of birth there is an objective danger to the preservation of life; we know what that means in the reality sense. But psychologically it has no meaning at all. The danger attending birth has still no psychic content. For certainly we cannot imagine as existing in the fœtus anything which in the least approaches any sort of knowledge of the possibility of death as an outcome. The fœtus can be aware of nothing beyond a gross disturbance in the economy of its narcissistic libido. Large amounts of excitation press upon it, giving rise to novel sensations of unpleasure; numerous organs enforce increased cathexes in their behalf, as it were a prelude to the object-cathexis soon to be initiated; what is there in all this that can be regarded as bearing the stamp of a "danger situation"?

Unfortunately, we know far too little of the mental make-up of the newborn to be able to answer such a question directly. I cannot even vouch for the usefulness of the description I have just given. It is easy to say that the newborn infant will repeat the affect of anxiety in every situation which reminds

it of the birth situation. The real question, however, is by what and of what it is reminded.

There is left us hardly any other course to pursue
than to study the occasions on which the infant or
the slightly older child gives evidence of a readiness
to develop anxiety. In his book, *The Trauma of
Birth,* Rank has made a very vigorous attempt to
demonstrate a relationship between the earliest
phobias of the child and the impression which the
birth experience has made upon it, but I cannot
consider the attempt a very happy one. Two criti-
cisms can be brought against it, of which the first
is that it makes the assumption that in the process
of birth the child has been the recipient of sense
impressions, particularly visual ones, the renewal
of which may evoke the memory of the birth trauma
and therewith a reaction of anxiety. This assumption is entirely unproved and very improbable; it
is not credible that the child has preserved any
other than tactile and general sensations from the
act of birth. If, then, the child later shows a fear of
small animals which disappear into holes or come
out of them, Rank explains this reaction as its perception of an analogy which, however, would not
strike the child. Secondly, in appraising these later

anxiety situations Rank holds responsible the memory either of the happy existence within the uterus or of its traumatic disturbance, entirely according to the necessities of the case, thus throwing the door wide open to arbitrariness of interpretation. Individual instances of this childhood anxiety flatly contradict the Rankian principle. If the child is brought into darkness and solitude, we should expect that it would welcome this restoration of the intrauterine situation; and if the fact that in precisely these circumstances the child reacts with anxiety is ascribed to the memory of the interruption of that happy state through birth, one may be pardoned for failing to appreciate the appositeness of such reasoning.

I am forced to the conclusion that the earliest phobias of childhood do not permit of being directly traced to the impression made upon the child by the act of birth, and that they have thus far, in fact, defied all explanation. A certain predisposition to anxiety on the part of the infant is indubitable. It is not at its maximum immediately after birth, to diminish gradually thereafter, but first makes its appearance later on with the progress of psychic development, and persists over a certain period of childhood. When early phobias of this sort continue beyond such a period, they give rise to the suspicion of a neurotic disturbance, although their relationship to the definite neuroses of later childhood is in no wise clear.

Only a few instances of the expression of anxiety in infancy are intelligible to us; we shall have to keep to these. Thus, the three situations of being left alone, being in the dark, and finding a strange person in place of the one in whom the child has confidence (the mother), are all reducible to a single situation, that of feeling the loss of the loved (longed for) person. From this point forwards the way is clear to an understanding of anxiety and to the reconciling of the contradictions which seem to be connected with it.

The memory picture of the person longed for is certainly cathected in very intense degree, probably at first in hallucinatory fashion. But this is without result, and now it appears as if this longing were transformed into anxiety. It decidedly seems as if this anxiety were an expression of helplessness, as if the still very undeveloped creature did not know what else to do with his longing. Anxiety thus seems to be a reaction to the perception of the absence of the object, and there at once spring to mind the analogies that castration anxiety has also separation from a highly valued object as its content and that the most basic anxiety of all, the "primal anxiety" of birth, arises in connection with separation from the mother.

The next consideration takes us beyond this emphasis upon loss of the object. If the infant longs for the sight of the mother, it does so, surely, only because it already knows from experience that she gratifies all its needs without delay. The situation which the infant appraises as "danger," and against which it desires reassurance, is therefore one of not being gratified, of an *increase of tension arising from non-gratification of its needs*—a situation against which it is powerless. I believe that from this standpoint everything falls into place; the situation of privation, in which stimuli reach an unpleasurable magnitude and intensity without an ability to cope with them psychically and thus provide for their discharge, must represent to the infant a situation analogous to the birth experience, a repetition of the danger situation; what the two situations have in common is the economic disturbance brought about by an increase in stimuli demanding some disposition made of them, this common factor hence being the very essence of the "danger." In both cases the reaction of anxiety appears, a reaction which still in the infant proves to the purpose since the discharge of the anxiety via the respiratory and vocal musculature now calls the mother to the infant's side, just as earlier it aroused respiratory activity to get rid of internal stimuli. More than this sign of danger the child does not need to have preserved from birth.

Along with the experiencing of the fact that an external and perceptible object may put an end to the danger situation reminiscent of birth, there takes place a displacement of the content of the danger from the economic situation to that which occasions it, namely, object loss. The perception of the absence of the mother now becomes the danger at the appearance of which the infant gives the signal of anxiety, even before the economic situation which is feared has arisen. This change represents a first great step in advance in the economy of self-preservation, and includes at the same time the transition from the automatically unpurposed creation *de novo* of anxiety to its purposeful reproduction as a signal of danger.

In both respects, alike as an automatic phenomenon and as a safety signal, anxiety proves to be a product of the psychic helplessness of the infant which is the obvious counterpart of its biological helplessness. The striking coincidence that both birth anxiety and the anxiety of the infant alike claim separation from the mother as their prerequisite needs no psychological interpretation; it is simply enough explicable biologically by the fact that the mother, who in the beginning had satisfied all the needs of the fœtus through her body mechanisms, continues after birth as well to exercise in some measure this same function, although by other means. Intrauterine life and early infancy form a continuum to a far greater extent than the striking cæsura of the act of birth would lead us to believe. The psychic mother object replaces for the child the biological fœtal situation. Hence we should not forget that during intrauterine life the mother was not an object, and that there were no objects at all at that period.

It is easy to see that in this continuum there is no room for an abreacting of the birth trauma, and that any other function of anxiety than that of a signal for avoiding a situation of danger is not discoverable. Object loss as the precondition of anxiety now has some further implications. For the next transformation of anxiety, the castration anxiety which makes its appearance in the phallic phase, is a separation anxiety also, and is similarly

conditioned. The danger here is separation from
the genital. A seemingly entirely legitimate line of
thought of Ferenczi's enables us to recognize clearly
here the point of connection with the earlier content of the danger situation. The high narcissistic
value attaching to the penis may be referable to
the fact that the possession of this organ contains
a guaranty of reunion with the mother (or mother
substitute) in the act of coitus. Deprivation of this
member is tantamount to a second separation from
the mother, and thus has again the significance (as
in the case of birth) of being delivered over helpless to the unpleasurable tension arising from the
non-gratification of a need. This need, of which the
increase is feared, is now, however, a specialized
one, a need of the genital libido, and no longer an
undifferentiated one, as in infancy. I would add
here that the fantasy of returning to the uterus is the
substitute for coitus which we find in impotent
men (those inhibited by the threat of castration).
In the spirit of Ferenczi's formulation one may say
that the individual who wished to have his genital
organ act as a proxy in his return to the uterus in
fact regressively substitutes for this organ his whole
body.

The various steps in the development of the

child, its increased independence, the sharper differentiation of its mental apparatus into various
agencies, the appearance of its new needs—all these
cannot remain without their effect upon the content of the danger situation. We have followed
the change in the content of the latter from loss of
the maternal object to castration, and we now see the
next step therein as caused by the power of the
superego. With the impersonalization of the parental authority at whose hands castration was
feared, the danger becomes more indefinite. Fear
of castration develops into dread of conscience, into
social anxiety. It is now no longer easy to state what
it is that there is fear of. The formula, "separation,
exclusion from the horde," applies only to that
more lately developed portion of the superego
which was patterned after social models, not to the
nucleus thereof which corresponds to the intro-
jected parental authority. Expressed in more general terms, it is the anger, the punishment, of the
superego, the loss of its love, which the ego appre-
hends as a danger and to which it responds with the
signal of anxiety. The final transformation undergone by this fear of the superego has appeared to me
to consist of death- (life-) anxiety, fear felt for the

projection of the superego upon the powers of destiny.

Formerly I attached a certain value to the proposition that the cathexis withdrawn in repression finds employment as a discharge in the form of anxiety. This seems to me today of very little interest. The difference consists in the fact that formerly I believed anxiety to originate in every instance automatically through an economic process, whereas the present conception of anxiety as a signal intended by the ego for the purpose of influencing the pleasure-pain mechanism renders us independent of this economic restriction. It does not contradict this supposition, of course, that for the arousing of affect the ego employs precisely the energy set free by the withdrawal of cathexis in repression, but it has become unimportant to distinguish with which moiety of energy this is accomplished.

Another assertion I once made now demands re-examination in the light of our new conception. I refer to the statement that the ego is the real seat of anxiety; I think that this statement will prove to be correct. That is to say, we have no reason to ascribe any expression of anxiety to the superego. But when it is a matter of an "anxiety of the id," one does not have so much to contradict this as to emend an infelicitous expression. Anxiety is an affective state which can of course be experienced only by the ego. The id cannot be afraid, as the ego can; it is not an organization, and cannot estimate situations of danger. On the contrary, it is of extremely frequent occurrence that processes are initiated or executed in the id which give the ego occasion to develop anxiety; as a matter of fact, the repressions which are probably the earliest are motivated, like the majority of all later ones, by such fear on the part of the ego of this or that process in the id. We have good grounds here for once again distinguishing the two cases: that in which something happens in the id which activates one of the danger situations to which the ego is sensitive, causing the latter to give the anxiety signal for inhibition; and that in which there develops in the id a situation analogous to the birth trauma, which automatically brings about a reaction of anxiety. The two cases are brought into closer approximation to each other if it is emphasized that the second corresponds to the initial and original situation of danger, whereas the first corresponds to one of the anxiety-occasioning situations subsequently derived from it. Or, to relate the matter to actually existing disorders: the second case is that which is operative in the ætiology of the "actual" neuroses, the first is characteristic of the psychoneuroses.

We now see that we need not dismiss earlier formulations as without value but have merely to bring them into line with our newer understanding. It is undeniable that in abstinence, in perverted interference with the normal discharge of sexual excitation, or in the diverting of the latter from its psychic elaboration, anxiety arises directly out of libido; that is to say, there is brought about that state of helplessness of the ego in the face of excessive tension arising from ungratified need which results, as in birth, in the development of anxiety, so that there is again a possibility, which although obvious is of no great consequence, that it is precisely the excess of unutilized libido that finds its discharge in the form of anxiety. We know that psychoneuroses develop with particular readiness on the basis of these "actual" neuroses; and this may mean that the ego makes attempts to minimize and to fix by means of symptoms the anxiety which it has learned to hold temporarily in suspension. Probably analysis of the traumatic war neuroses (although this term includes a wide variety of disorders, certainly) would have shown that a certain proportion of them share the characteristics of "actual" neuroses.

When we represented the various danger situations as developing out of the original prototype of birth, we were far from maintaining that every later anxiety-occasioning situation simply renders inoperative those which were earlier effective in giving rise to anxiety. The progressive development of the ego contributes, it is true, to depriving of value and relegating to unimportance the earlier danger situation, so that it may be said that to a given period of development is assigned the anxiety-occasioning situation which is, so to speak, appropriate to it. Psychic helplessness is the danger which is consonant with the period of immaturity of the ego, as object loss is the danger appertaining to the state of dependence of early childhood, the danger of castration to the phallic phase, and dread of the superego to the latency period. And yet all these danger situations and anxiety determinants may persist alongside one another and cause the ego to react with anxiety at a later period also than the appropriate one; or several of them may become operative simultaneously. Possibly there also exists a close relationship between the danger situation which is effective in the given case and the form of the neurosis which develops in consequence.[1]

When in an earlier chapter of this inquiry we encountered the significance of the danger of castration in more than one neurotic disorder, we warned

[1] Since the differentiation between the ego and the id was made, our interest in the problems of repression has necessarily undergone a revival. Until then we were satisfied to dwell upon those of its elements which are referable to the ego—namely, the keeping of the repressed material out of consciousness and its withholding from motor discharge, and the creating of substitute (symptom) formations; of the repressed instinctual impulse itself we assumed that it persisted unchanged for an indefinite period in the unconscious. Now our interest shifts to the fate of the repressed, and we begin to feel that this persistence, unchanged and unchanging, is not a matter of course, is perhaps not even the rule. The original impulse has in any case been inhibited and deflected from its aim. But has its root persisted in the unconscious, having proved resistant to the modifying and depreciatory influence of life? Do there therefore still exist the old desires, of the earlier existence of which analysis informs us? The answer appears obvious and certain: The old repressed desires must still persist in the unconscious, since we find their lineal descendants, the symptoms, still active. But this answer is inadequate; it does not make it possible to distinguish between the two possibilities that, on the one hand, the old desire now operates only through its descendants, to which it has transferred all its cathectic energy, or, on the other hand, that the desire itself persists in addition. If it was its destiny to be expended in the cathexis of its descendants, there remains the third possibility that in the course of the neurosis the wish was reactivated through regression, so out of accord with the present may it be. One need not regard these considerations as otiose; there is much in the phenomena of both the morbid and the normal life of the psyche which seems to demand the raising of such questions. In my study of the breakdown of the œdipus complex I became mindful of the distinction between the mere repression and the true disappearance of an old desire or impulse.

ourselves against overestimating this factor, since
it assuredly could not be the crucial one in the
female sex, the sex certainly more predisposed to
neurosis. We see now that we are in no danger of
taking castration anxiety to be the sole motive force
behind the defense processes resulting in neurosis.
I have explained elsewhere how the development
of the little girl is guided to tender object-cathexis
through the castration complex. It is precisely in the
female that object loss seems to remain the most
effective situation of danger. As to that which gives
rise to her anxiety, we may introduce the slight
modification that it is no longer a matter of feeling
the absence, or of the loss in reality, of the object,
but rather of the loss of the object's love. Since it
is certainly true that hysteria has a greater affinity
with femininity, just as compulsion neurosis has
with masculinity, the idea suggests itself that, as a
determinant of anxiety, loss of love plays a rôle in
hysteria similar to that of the threat of castration in
the phobias and of dread of the superego in compulsion neurosis.

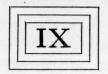

The Relation between
Symptom and Anxiety

IT NOW remains to deal with the relationship between symptom formation and the development
of anxiety. Two opinions about this seem to be
prevalent. One of them terms the anxiety itself a
symptom of the neurosis, the other conceives of a far
more intimate connection between the two. According to this latter view, all symptom formation would
be brought about solely in order to avoid anxiety;
the symptoms bind the psychic energy which otherwise would be discharged as anxiety, so that anxiety
would be the fundamental phenomenon and the
central problem of neurosis.

The at least partial justification of this second
position can be supplied by means of certain striking examples. If an agoraphobic who has been accompanied whenever he went out on the street is
left alone there, he produces an attack of anxiety;
if a compulsion neurotic is prevented from washing

his hands after touching something, he becomes a prey to almost insupportable anxiety. It is clear, therefore, that the stipulation of being accompanied and the compulsion to wash has as their purpose, and also their result, the averting of an outbreak of anxiety. In this sense, every inhibition also that the ego imposes on itself can be termed a symptom.

Since we have reduced the development of anxiety to a response to situations of danger, we shall prefer to say that the symptoms are created in order to remove or rescue the ego from the situation of danger. If symptom formation is prevented, then the danger actually makes its appearance—that is to say, a situation analogous to birth comes about, a situation in which the ego finds itself helpless against the ever-increasing strength of the instinctual demand in question; in other words, we have present the first and earliest of the determinants of anxiety. For our point of view the relationships between anxiety and symptom prove to be less close than was supposed, the result of our having interposed between the two the factor of the danger situation. We can also say, in supplement to this, that the development of anxiety induces symptom formation—nay more, it is a *sine qua non* thereof, for if the ego did not forcibly arouse the pleasure-pain mechanism through the development of anxiety, it would not acquire the power to put a stop to the danger-threatening process elaborated in the id. At the same time there is an obvious tendency on the part of the ego to restrict the development of anxiety to a minimum, to employ anxiety only as a signal, for otherwise there would merely be experienced somewhere else the unpleasure threatened by the instinctual process—a result which would not accord with the purpose of the pleasure principle, although often enough coming about, it is true, in the neuroses.

Symptom formation thus has the actual result of putting an end to the danger situation. It has two aspects: one of them, which remains concealed from us, causes in the id that alteration by means of which the ego is preserved from danger; the other, visible to us, reveals what it has created in place of the instinctual process thus modified, namely, substitute formation.

We should express ourselves more accurately, however, if we ascribed to the process of defense what we have just said of symptom formation, and used the term symptom formation itself as synonymous with substitute formation. It then seems evident that the defensive process is analogous to

flight, by means of which the ego avoids a danger
threatening from without, and that it represents,
indeed, an attempt at flight from an instinctual
danger. The considerations which weigh against
this comparison will themselves prove illuminating.
In the first place, the objection might be raised
that object loss (loss of the object's love) and the
threat of castration are just as much dangers threatening from without as is for example a ravening
beast, and are therefore not instinctual dangers. Yet
the case is not at all the same. The wolf would probably attack us, regardless of how we behaved towards
it; but the beloved person would not withdraw his
love, we should not be threatened with castration,
if we did not cherish within ourselves certain feelings and desires. Thus it is these instinctual impulses which become the precondition of the external danger, its *conditio sine qua non,* and thereby
themselves a source of danger; and we can now com-
bat the external danger by measures taken against
dangers from within. In the animal phobias the
danger seems still to be perceived entirely as an external one, just as in the symptom also it undergoes
an external displacement. In compulsion neurosis
the danger is to a far greater degree internalized;
that part of the fear of the superego which may be

called social anxiety still represents an internal substitute for an external danger, while the other part,
fear of conscience, is entirely endopsychic.

A second objection would be to the effect that in
the attempt to escape from a threatening external
danger all that we do, in fact, is to increase the
distance in space between us and that which threatens. We do not put ourselves in an attitude of defense against the danger, we do not try to change
anything in the danger itself, as would be the case
if we attacked the wolf with a club or shot at it with
a gun. But the defensive process seems to go beyond
what would correspond merely to an attempt at
flight; it actually interferes with the threatening instinctual process, suppresses it somehow, deflects it
from its aim, and thereby renders it harmless. This
objection appears to be a very cogent one, and one
we shall have to take into account. We believe it
may well be that there are defensive processes which
can with justice be compared to an attempt at
flight, while in the case of others the ego offers resistance of a far more active kind, undertaking
vigorous counteractive measures. But it is possible
that the comparison of defense with flight is rendered untenable by the fact that the ego and the
instinctual drive in the id are in fact parts of the

same organization, and do not have, as the wolf and the child do, a separate existence from each other; so that every form of behavior on the part of the ego must have a modifying influence upon the instinctual process.

Through the study of the situations which occasion anxiety we have had to envisage with what might be called rational idealization the behavior of the ego in defense. Every danger situation corresponds to a given period of life or stage of development of the psyche, to which it appears appropriate. In early infancy the organism is not really equipped to cope psychically with large amounts of excitation reaching it from without or within. At a certain period of life it is in actual fact to the individual's greatest interest that the persons upon whom he is dependent shall not withdraw their tender care. When the boy perceives the powerful father as his rival for the mother and becomes aware of his aggressive tendencies against his father and his sexual desires towards his mother, he is quite right in being afraid of him; and the fear of being punished by him may, when reënforced phylogenetically, be expressed as fear of castration. On his becoming a social being, fear of the superego, conscience, becomes a necessity, omission of this step the source

of severe conflicts and dangers. But at this point a
new problem enters.

Let us for the moment try the experiment of substituting for the affect of anxiety some other affect,
for example that of grief. We consider it entirely
normal that a little girl should weep bitterly at the
age of four if her doll is broken, at the age of six
if her teacher reprimands her, at the age of sixteen
if her sweetheart neglects her, at the age of twenty-
five, perhaps, if she buries her child. Each of these
grief-occasioning situations has its proper time and
vanishes with its passing; but the later and more
definite ones remain operative throughout life. We
should be rather surprised, in fact, if this girl, after
she had become a wife and mother, should weep
over some knickknack getting broken. Yet this is
how neurotics behave. Although in their mental
apparatus there have long since developed all the
agencies necessary for dealing with a wide range of
stimuli, although they are mature enough to be able
to gratify the greater part of their needs themselves,
although they know perfectly well that castration
is no longer practised as a punishment, they nevertheless behave as though the old danger situation
still existed, they remain under the spell of all the
old causes of anxiety.

The answer to all this will prove somewhat prolix, for it will have in the first place to sift the actual facts of the case. In a large number of instances the old causes of anxiety have in reality become inoperative, but only after having first brought neurotic reactions into existence. The morbid fear of being alone, of the dark, and of strangers, on the part of the smallest children, which is almost to be labelled normal, disappears for the most part at a somewhat later age; such fears are "outgrown," as we say of many other disturbances of childhood. The phobias of animals so frequently met with share this same fate; many of the conversion hysterias of childhood are not carried over into later life. In the latency period the practice of ceremonials is of extremely frequent occurrence, yet only a very small percentage of these cases later develop a full-blown compulsion neurosis. The neuroses of children, so far at least as concerns upper-class urban children of the white race, are regularly occurring episodes in development, although too little attention is still paid to them. In not a single adult neurotic do the indications of a childhood neurosis fail of occurrence, while on the other hand by no means all children who show them become neurotic subsequently. Therefore in the course of growing up the anxiety-determinants which once existed must have been relinquished, the situations originally endowed with danger have lost their significance. To this must be added that certain of these danger situations survive into a later period of life by means of a modification, in keeping with that later period, of the character of what gives rise to anxiety. Thus, for example, castration anxiety persists in the guise of syphilophobia, after it has been learned that castration is no longer customary as a punishment for giving the sexual appetites free rein but that serious diseases threaten instinctual freedom instead. Certain other of the things that occasion anxiety are destined not to disappear at all, but are to accompany the human being throughout life, such as, for example, the fear of the superego. The neurotic is then distinguished from the normal person in that his response to these dangers is disproportionately increased. Yet against the return of the original traumatic anxiety situation even maturity offers after all no adequate protection; there may exist for every one a limit beyond which his psyche fails in the attempt to cope with the demands which the excitation in question makes upon him.

These minor reservations cannot possibly be taken as militating against the fact which we have been discussing: the fact, namely, that in their response to danger so many people remain infantile, continuing to react with anxiety to situations which should have long ceased to evoke it; to dispute this would be to deny the very fact of neurosis, for it is exactly such persons whom we call neurotics. But how does this situation come about? Why are not all neuroses merely episodes in the individual's development which become a closed chapter when the next stage of development is reached? Whence comes the element of permanency in these reactions to danger? Whence springs the preference over all other affects which the affect of anxiety seems to enjoy in alone evoking reactions which we distinguish from others as abnormal and which in their inexpediency obstruct the stream of life? In other words, we find ourselves abruptly confronted once again by the oft-repeated riddle: What is the source of neurosis, what is its ultimate, its specific, underlying principle? After decades of analytic effort this problem rises up before us, as untouched as at the beginning.

The Birth Trauma: A Critique

ANXIETY is the reaction to danger. One cannot escape the thought, indeed, that the very nature of danger has a bearing upon the fact that the affect of anxiety is able to command pride of place in the mental economy. But the dangers in question are those common to all mankind; they are the same for everybody; so that what we need and do not have at our disposal is some factor which shall enable us to understand the basis of selection of those individuals who are able to subject the affect of anxiety, despite its singularity, to normal psychic control, or which on the other hand determines those who must prove unequal to this task. I have in mind two attempts which have been made to discover such a factor; and certainly any such attempt may reasonably expect a sympathetic reception, since it promises to remedy a crying need. The two attempts I refer to supplement each other in that they attack the problem from opposite ends. The first was undertaken more than ten years ago [1] by Alfred Adler; his thesis, in a nutshell, is that those individuals fail to solve the problem which danger imposes in whom an organ inferiority makes such a task too difficult of accomplishment. Now if it were true that *simplex sigillum veri,* one would welcome such a solution as this as a very salvation. On the contrary, however, the consensus of criticism during the decade just passed has amply demonstrated the complete inadequacy of this explanation, which, moreover, totally disregards the wealth of facts discovered by psychoanalysis.

The second attempt was undertaken by Otto Rank in 1923 in his book, *The Trauma of Birth.* It would be invidious to compare this attempt with Adler's in any other respect than the single one here emphasized, for Rank's rests on a psychoanalytic foundation, pursues psychoanalytic trends of thought, and is to be regarded as a legitimate effort towards the solution of analytic problems. In the relation between the individual and danger Rank assigns less importance to organ inferiority in the individual and emphasizes rather the varying intensity of the danger. The process of birth constitutes the first danger situation, the economic up-

---

[1] Now more than twenty years ago.—TRANSLATOR'S NOTE.

heaval which birth entails becomes the prototype
of the anxiety reaction; we have already followed
out the line of development which connects this
first danger, this first anxiety-occasioning situation,
with all subsequent ones; and in so doing we saw
that they all retain something in common in that all
of them signify in some sense a separation from the
mother, at first only in a biological respect, then in
the sense of a direct object loss, and later of an object loss mediated in indirect ways. The revealing
of this sequence of events is an undisputed merit of
the Rankian construction. Now the trauma of birth
affects different individuals with differing intensity,
the intensity of the anxiety reaction varies with the
severity of the trauma, and, according to Rank, it is
supposed to depend upon the degree to which this
initial development of anxiety takes place whether
the individual ever succeeds in gaining control over
it, whether he becomes a neurotic or a normal person.

The detailed criticism of Rank's thesis is not our
task, but merely its examination from the standpoint of its serviceability in the solution of our
problem. Rank's formula, that those persons become neurotic who on account of the severity of the
birth trauma have never succeeded in abreacting it

completely, is theoretically open to the greatest possible doubt. It is not entirely clear what is meant by the abreacting of the trauma. If it is taken literally, one arrives at the quite untenable conclusion that the neurotic approaches more and more closely to a state of health the more frequently and the more intensively he reproduces the affect of anxiety. It was on the ground of this very nonconformity with reality that I abandoned, indeed, the theory of abreaction, the theory which played so large a part in catharsis. The emphasis upon the varying severity of the birth trauma leaves no room for the legitimate ætiological claim of constitutional factors. This severity is an organic factor, certainly, one which compared with constitution is a chance factor, and is itself dependent upon many influences which are to be termed accidental, such as for example timely obstetrical assistance. But the Rankian theory has left constitutional as well as phylogenetic factors entirely out of account. If one were to allow for the importance of a constitutional factor, such as via the modification that it would depend much more upon how extensively the individual reacts to the variable severity of the birth trauma, one would deprive the theory of meaning and have reduced the new factor which Rank has introduced to a subordinate rôle. That which determines whether or not neurosis is the outcome lies, then, in some other area, and once again in an unknown one.

The fact that the human being shares the birth process with other mammals, whereas a particular disposition to neurosis is the special privilege which he alone possesses, hardly speaks very strongly in favor of the Rankian theory. The principal objection to be raised against it, however, remains the fact that it hangs in mid-air, instead of being based upon verified observation. For no trustworthy investigation has ever been carried out to determine whether difficult and protracted birth is correlated in indisputable fashion with the development of neurosis— indeed, whether children whose birth has been of this character manifest even the nervousness of earliest infancy for a longer period or more intensely than others. If the assertion is made that precipitate births, those easy for the mother, may possibly have for the child the significance of a severe trauma, then *a fortiori* it would certainly be necessary that births resulting in asphyxia should produce beyond any doubt the consequences alleged. It seems an advantage of the Rankian ætiology that it postulates a factor capable of being checked empirically; but as long as such a check has never actually been undertaken, it is impossible to estimate its real value.

On the other hand, I cannot share the view that the Rankian theory controverts the ætiological importance of the sexual instincts as this has so far been recognized in psychoanalysis; for the theory refers only to the behavior of the individual towards the danger situation, and leaves the matter open whether the person who was unable to overcome the initial dangers which beset him will necessarily fail in the situations of sexual danger of later occurrence and thereby be forced into neurosis.

All in all, then, I do not believe that Rank's endeavor has supplied us with the solution of the problem of the fundamental basis of neurosis, and I think that it cannot yet be decided how large a contribution to the solution of the problem it actually makes. If investigation of the influence of difficult birth upon the disposition to neurosis yields only a negative result, its contribution will be slight indeed. I am very much afraid that the need for a tangible and simple "ultimate cause" of neurosis is doomed to remain ungratified. The ideal possibility, for which probably even today the physician longs, would be that of a bacillus which can be isolated and grown in pure culture and the inoculation of which produces the identical effect in every individual; or, somewhat less fantastically, the evolving of chemical substances, the administration of which produces a given neurosis or abolishes it. But probability is hardly on the side of such solutions of the problem.

Psychoanalysis yields less simple, less satisfying intelligence. I have here to repeat only what has long been familiar, adding nothing new. When the ego has succeeded in defending itself against a dangerous instinctual impulse, as for example by the mechanism of repression, it has inhibited and inflicted damage upon that portion of the id but has at the same time also given it a bit of independence and renounced a bit of its own sovereignty. This follows from the nature of repression, which is, at bottom, an attempt at flight. The repressed material is now "outlawed," excluded from the great organization of the ego, subject only to the laws which prevail in the domain of the unconscious. If now the danger situation is altered, so that the ego is without incentive to defend itself against a newly arisen instinctual impulse analogous to the one which has been repressed, the consequences of this limitation of the ego's sovereignty become manifest. The new instinct pursues its course in automatic fashion—I should prefer to say, under the influence of the repetition compulsion; it follows the same path as did the instinct which had previously been repressed, as though the successfully surmounted danger situation were still in existence. The fixating factor in repression is thus the repetition compulsion of the unconscious id, which normally is put an end to only through freely mobile ego-functioning. Now the ego may occasionally succeed in making a breach in the barriers of repression which it has itself set up, in reacquiring its influence over the instinctual impulse and in guiding the course of the new instinctual impulse in accordance with the altered danger situation. But as a matter of fact the ego often fails in this and is unable to undo its repressions. Quantitative factors may play a deciding part in the outcome of this struggle. In many cases we have the impression that the outcome is a compulsory one; the regressive attraction exerted by the repressed impulse and the force of the repression are so great that the new impulse can only follow out the repetition compulsion. In other cases we perceive the contribution of another set of forces; the attraction exerted by the repressed prototype is re-enforced by the repulsion exerted by reality obstacles which oppose any other discharge of the newly arisen instinctual impulse.

That this is the course of events in the fixation of repression, and in the retention of danger situations no longer current, receives its proof from the fact of analytic therapy, a fact modest enough in itself but theoretically scarcely to be overestimated. When in analysis we render the ego assistance enabling it to undo its repressions, the ego regains its power over the repressed id and can so steer the course of the instinctual impulses as if the old danger situations no longer existed. What we achieve in this way is in complete harmony with what we accomplish in other spheres of medical activity. As a rule our treatment has to be satisfied with bringing about more rapidly, more certainly and with less trouble the satisfactory outcome which under favorable conditions would have resulted spontaneously.

The foregoing considerations tell us that there are quantitative elements not directly evident but to be apprehended only *a posteriori,* which decide the question whether the old danger situations are adhered to, whether the repressions effected by the ego are preserved, whether childhood neuroses are carried over into later life, or not. Of the factors which are contributory in the causation of neurosis, the factors which have created the conditions under which the forces of the psyche contend among themselves, there are three which present themselves for our consideration—a biological, a phylogenetic, and a purely psychological factor. The biological factor is the protracted helplessness and dependence of the young of the human species. The intrauterine life of the human being seems to be relatively abbreviated as compared with that of the majority of animals; the human infant is sent into the world more unfinished than the young of the latter. For this reason the influence of the external environment is intensified, the differentiating of the ego from the id is promoted very early, the dangers which the environment presents are increased in importance, and the value attached to the object who alone can offer protection against these dangers and effect a substitution for the intrauterine life which has been lost, is enormously augmented. This biological factor of helplessness thus brings into being the first situations of danger and creates the need to be loved which the human being is destined never to renounce.

The second, the phylogenetic, factor is one which we merely infer; but a very remarkable fact of libido development has compelled us to assume its existence. We find that the sexual life of the human being does not develop in progressive fashion from incipience to maturity, as in the case of most of the closely related animals, but that it suffers an abrupt interruption after an initial early florescence extending to about the fifth year, after which it commences anew with puberty, dovetailing, as it were, with the tendencies of the infantile period. We believe that something momentous to the destinies of the human species must have taken place which has left behind as an historical precipitate this interruption of sexual development. The pathogenic importance of this phenomenon accrues from the fact that most of the instinctual demands of this infantile sexuality are treated as dangers and guarded against by the ego, so that the sexual impulses of puberty, which should be ego-compatible, are in danger of succumbing to the attraction exerted by their infantile prototypes and of following them into repression. It is here that we come upon the most definite ætiology of the neuroses. It is noteworthy that early contact with the demands of sexuality has the same effect upon the ego as premature contact with the environment.

The third or psychological factor is to be found in an imperfection of our psychic apparatus which is connected with its differentiation into ego and id and hence which is traceable also, in the last analysis, to the influence of the environment. By reason of the dangers which reality offers, the ego is compelled to adopt an attitude of defense towards certain instinctual impulses in the id, to treat them as dangers. But the ego cannot protect itself against internal instinctual dangers so effectively as against a piece of reality which is strange to it. Itself intimately connected with the id, the ego is able to stave off an instinctual danger only by putting restrictions upon its own organization and by tolerating symptom formation as a substitute for its crippling of the instinct. If then the press of the repudiated instinct is renewed, there result for the ego all the difficulties which we know as neurotic suffering.

Further than this, I must believe, our insight into the nature and causation of neurosis has not at the present time progressed.

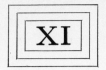

Addenda

IN THE course of the foregoing remarks a number of topics were touched upon which had to be dismissed prematurely, but which shall now be brought together in order that they may receive the share of attention which is their due.

A. Certain Modifications of Views Previously Held

(a) Resistance and Anticathexis

It is an important element of the theory of repression that this process is not one which takes place on a single occasion but is one demanding a continuous expenditure of effort. Should this effort be intermitted, the repressed impulse, which receives a continuous influx from its sources of origin, would thereupon strike out upon the same path off which it had been forced, and the repression would have failed of its purpose or would have to be repeated

an indefinite number of times. Thus from the unin-
terrupted character of the instinctual impulse there
arises the demand on the ego to insure its defense by
an unremitting expenditure of effort. This action
for the protection of the repression is what we experience, in the course of our therapeutic efforts,
as *resistance*. Resistance presupposes what I have
termed *anticathexis*. Such an anticathexis is evident
in compulsion neurosis. It there makes its appearance as an alteration of the ego, as a reaction formation in the ego, through an intensification of the
attitude which is the antithesis of the instinctual
tendency to be repressed (pity, conscientiousness,
cleanliness). These reaction formations in compulsion neurosis are all of them exaggerations of normal
character traits developed during the latency period.
It is much more difficult to demonstrate anticathexis
in hysteria, where, theoretically, it is just as indispensable. In hysteria, too, a certain amount of ego-
alteration through reaction formation is evident, in
many circumstances becoming so striking that it
claims attention as the cardinal symptom in the clinical syndrome. In this manner, for example, the
ambivalency conflict in hysteria is resolved; hate for
a loved person is kept submerged by an excess of
tenderness towards him and of anxious concern

about him. As a point of difference from compulsion neurosis, however, one must emphasize the fact that such reaction formations do not manifest the general nature of character traits but are confined to quite specific situations. The hysterical woman, for example, who treats with excessive tenderness the children whom she really hates, does not on that account become more disposed to love in general than other women, not even more tender towards other children. The reaction formation of hysteria adheres tenaciously to a specific object and is not elevated to the status of a general disposition of the ego. Of compulsion neurosis it is precisely this universalization, the looseness of object relationships, the displaceability marking object choice, which are characteristic.

Another type of anticathexis seems more consonant with the specific nature of hysteria. The repressed instinctual impulse may be activated (recathected) from two directions: from within, through an increase in strength of the instinct in question, an increase derived from its internal sources of excitation; or from without, through the perception of an object desired by the instinct. Now the hysterical type of anticathexis is predominantly directed outwards, against the dangerous perception; it takes the form of a special watchfulness which, through restrictions imposed upon the ego, avoids situations in which such a perception would inevitably occur, and which effects the withdrawal of attention from the perception if this has actually occurred. Certain French writers (for example, Laforgue) have recently designated this process observed in hysteria by the special term "scotomization." Even more strikingly than in hysteria is this technique of anticathexis displayed in the phobias, the interest of which is concentrated upon effecting a further and further removal of the possibility of experiencing the dreaded perception. The contrast in the direction of the anticathexis as between hysteria and phobia on the one hand and compulsion neurosis on the other appears to be of importance, even though this antithesis is not an absolute one. It leads us to suppose that a rather intimate connection exists between repression and external anticathexis, as well as between regression and internal anticathexis (ego-alteration through reaction formation). Defense against dangerous perceptions is, moreover, a general task of neurosis. The various commands and prohibitions of compulsion neurosis presumably serve the same purpose.

We have already made it clear that the resistance

which we have to overcome in analysis is produced
by the ego, which clings tenaciously to its anti-
cathexes. The ego finds it difficult to turn its attention to perceptions and ideas the avoidance of which
it had until then made a rule, or to acknowledge as
belonging to it impulses which constitute the most
complete antithesis to those familiar to it as its own.
Our combating of resistance in the analysis is based
upon this conception of it. We make the resistance
conscious where, as so often, in consequence of its
connection with the repressed, it is unconscious; we
oppose logical arguments to it when or after it has
become conscious, promising the ego advantages
and rewards if it renounces the resistance. As regards the resistance of the ego there is therefore
nothing to call into question or to correct. On the
other hand, the question is whether resistance alone
covers the situation that confronts us in analysis.
We experience the fact that the ego still finds it difficult to nullify its repressions even after it has resolved to give up its resistances, and we have designated the phase of strenuous effort which follows
upon this laudable resolution as the period of
"working through." Now it is easy to recognize the
dynamic factor which makes this working through
necessary and intelligible. It can but be that after

the cessation of the ego-resistance there is still the power of the repetition compulsion, the attraction exerted by its unconscious prototypes upon the repressed instinctual process, to be overcome; nor is it in any way inconsistent with this to designate this factor as the *resistance of the unconscious.* Let us not grudge the effort necessary for such emendations; they are desirable if they enhance our understanding a little, and no discredit if they do not negative our previous conceptions but enrich them, perhaps make a generality more specific or broaden a conception which was too narrow.

It must not be supposed that through the foregoing emendation we have achieved a complete perspective regarding the kinds of resistance which confront us in analysis. When we go more deeply into the matter we note, rather, that we have five varieties of resistance to contend with, which derive from three sources, namely, from the ego, from the id, and from the superego—whereby the ego turns out to be the source of three forms of resistance differing from one another in their dynamics. The first of these three ego-resistances is the *repression* resistance just dealt with, about which there is least that is new to be said. From this form there is to be distinguished the transference resistance, which is

of the same character but which makes itself evident
in the analysis in other and far more definite ways,
since it has succeeded in creating a relationship to
the analytic situation or to the person of the analyst
and in reviving thereby, as if in the flesh, so to speak,
a repression which should be merely recalled. That
resistance is also an ego-resistance, although of quite
a different nature, which emanates from the *gain of
illness* and is based upon the inclusion of the symptom in the ego. It corresponds to opposition to the
renunciation of a gratification or a mode of relief.
The fourth variety of resistance—that of the id—we
have just now made responsible for the necessity of
working through. The fifth type of resistance, that
of the superego, the last recognized and the most
obscure, but not always the weakest, seems to derive
from the sense of guilt or need of punishment; it
resists any success and hence also recovery through
the analysis.

(b) Anxiety from Transformation of Libido

The conception of anxiety set forth in the present
work differs somewhat from that which previously
seemed to me to be legitimate. Formerly I considered anxiety a general reaction on the part of the
ego under conditions of unpleasure, I tried to ex-

plain its appearance on economic grounds exclusively, and, relying upon the results of investigation of the "actual" neuroses, I assumed that libido (sexual excitation) rejected by the ego or not utilized by it found direct discharge in the form of anxiety. But the fact cannot be overlooked that these various definitions do not accord very well with one another, or at least they do not follow necessarily from one another. Moreover, the appearance was given of an especially intimate relationship between anxiety and libido which again did not harmonize with the general character of anxiety as a reaction of unpleasure.

The objection to this conception arose out of the effort to make the ego the sole site of anxiety, and was thus one of the results of the articulation of the psychic apparatus attempted in *The Ego and the Id*. It was natural, in the earlier conception, to consider the libido of the repressed instinctual impulse the source of anxiety; according to the newer one, the ego, rather, was held responsible for this anxiety. We have, therefore, ego-anxiety or instinctual (id-) anxiety. Since the ego works with desexualized energy, the intimate connection between anxiety and libido was also loosened in the new version. I hope I have succeeded in at least clarifying the contradiction and in clearly demarcating the boundary lines of uncertainty.

Rank's reminder that the affect of anxiety is, as I myself at first maintained, a result of the birth process and a repetition of the situation lived through at that time, necessitated a reëxamination of the problem of anxiety. With his conception of birth as a trauma, of the anxiety state as a reaction of discharge thereof, and of every fresh occurrence of anxiety as an attempt to "abreact" the trauma more and more completely, I was unable to get further. There resulted the necessity of going back from the anxiety reaction to the *danger situation* behind it. With the introduction of this factor new points of view were presented for consideration. Birth became the prototype of all later danger situations which arose under the new conditions imposed by an altered form of existence and by the advance of psychic development. But its own significance was limited to this prototypic relationship to danger. The anxiety felt in the process of birth now became the prototype of an affective state which was obliged to share the fate of other affects. It was reproduced either automatically in situations which were analogous to that of its origin and as an inexpedient type of reaction, after having been an appropriate

one in the initial situation of danger; or else the
ego acquired control over this affect and reproduced it itself, making use of it as a warning of danger and as a means of rousing into action the
pleasure-pain mechanism. The biological significance of anxiety was validated by the recognizing of
anxiety as the universal reaction to the situation of
danger; the rôle of the ego as the site of anxiety
was confirmed by the granting to the ego of the
function of producing anxiety according to its needs.
To anxiety in later life were thus attributed two
modes of origin: the one involuntary, automatic,
economically justified whenever there arose a situation of danger analogous to birth; the other, produced by the ego when such a situation merely
threatened, in order to procure its avoidance. In
this second case the ego submitted to anxiety as to
a vaccination, so to speak, in order to escape a viru-
lent attack by means of an attenuated case of the
disease. In its unmistakable effort to limit the painful experience to an intimation, a signal, the ego
acted as if it had vividly pictured the danger situation. How the various danger situations develop in
succession and yet remain genetically linked with
one another has already been set forth in detail.
Perhaps we shall succeed in penetrating a little

further into the understanding of anxiety if we attack the problem of the relation between neurotic anxiety and true anxiety.

The direct transforming of libido into anxiety previously assumed has now become of less interest to us. If we do take it into consideration, we have several possibilities to differentiate. In the case of anxiety which the ego instigates as a signal, this transformation does not enter in, and thus plays no part in any of the danger situations which impel the ego to initiate a repression. The libidinal cathexis of the repressed instinctual impulse is put to another use, as is most clearly observable in conversion hysteria, than that of transformation into and discharge as anxiety. On the other hand, in our further discussion of the danger situation we shall encounter an instance of anxiety development which is probably to be regarded otherwise.

(c) *Repression and Defense*

In connection with the discussion of the problem of anxiety I resurrected a concept—or, more modestly expressed, a term—of which I made use exclusively when I first began my studies thirty years ago [1] but which I later dropped; I mean that of the process of

[1] Now forty years ago.—TRANSLATOR'S NOTE,

defense.[1] I substituted for it, later on, that of repression, but the relation between the two remained indefinite. I now think that it confers a distinct disadvantage to readopt the old concept of defense if in doing so it is laid down that this shall be the general designation for all the techniques of which the ego makes use in the conflicts which potentially lead to neurosis, while repression is the term reserved for one particular method of defense, one which because of the direction that our investigations took was the first with which we became acquainted.

Even a purely terminological innovation is justifiable if it is expressive of a new way of looking at the matter or of an extension of our insight. Now the readopting of the concept of defense and the restricting of that of repression takes into consideration a fact which has long been known but which has acquired additional significance through certain recent findings. We first met with repression and symptom formation in hysteria; we saw that the perceptual content of excitant experiences, the ideational content of pathogenic complexes, is forgotten and excluded from reproduction in memory, and we accordingly recognized in their withholding

[1] See *The Defense Neuro-psychoses*, Collected Papers, Vol. I.

from consciousness a cardinal characteristic of hysterical repression. Later we studied compulsion neurosis and found that in this disorder the pathogenic incidents are not forgotten. They remain conscious, but they become, in some manner which we still do not understand, "isolated," so that approximately the same result is attained as through hysterical amnesia. But the difference is great enough to justify our belief that the process by means of which the compulsion neurosis takes care of an instinctual demand could not be the same as in hysteria. Further investigation has shown us that in compulsion neurosis there is brought about, under the influence of the ego's opposition, a regression of the instinctual impulses to an earlier libidinal phase such as does not, it is true, make repression superfluous, but evidently operates to the same effect as repression. We have furthermore seen that the anticathexis which we assumed to be present in the case also of hysteria, plays in compulsion neurosis, in the form of reactive ego-alteration, a particularly large rôle in the protection of the ego; we have become cognizant of a process of "isolation," of the technique of which we can still give no account, which creates for itself a direct symptomatic expression, and likewise of what might be termed the magical procedure of "undoing," of the apotropaic trend of which there can be no doubt, but which has no further similarity to the process of "repression." These phenomena are sufficient reason for reintroducing the old concept of defense, which is able to embrace all these processes of similar purpose—namely, protection of the ego against instinctual demands—and for subsuming repression under this rubric as a special case thereof. The importance of such a nomenclature is increased if one considers the possibility that a deeper insight might reveal a close affinity between particular forms of defense and certain specific disorders, as for example between repression and hysteria. Our expectation even extends to the possibility of another important interrelationship. It may easily be that the psychic apparatus utilizes other methods of defense prior to the clear-cut differentiation of ego and id, prior to the erecting of a superego, than it does after these stages of organization have been attained.

B. Supplementary Remarks on Anxiety

There are certain characteristics possessed by the affect of anxiety, the investigation of which gives promise of further enlightenment. Anxiety is undeniably related to expectation; one feels anxiety *lest* something occur.[1] It is endowed with a certain character of indefiniteness and objectlessness; correct usage even changes its name when it has found an object, and in that case speaks instead of *dread*. Anxiety has, moreover, in addition to its relation to danger, a relation to neurosis, over the clarification of which we have expended much labor. For there arises the question why it is that not all anxiety reactions are neurotic, why we recognize so many of them as normal; and, finally, the distinction between true anxiety (*Realangst*) and neurotic anxiety needs to be properly evaluated.

Let us start with the latter task. The progress we have made has consisted in tracing a backward path from the reaction of anxiety to the situation of danger. If we apply the same process to the problem of true anxiety, its solution becomes simple. A *real* danger is a danger which we know, a true anxiety the anxiety in regard to such a known danger. Neurotic anxiety is anxiety in regard to a danger which we do not know. The neurotic danger must first be sought, therefore: analysis has taught us that it is an instinctual danger. By bringing into con-

---

[1] That is, the German usage is: *Angst* vor *etwas*—literally, anxiety *before* something, instead of *of* something.—TRANSLATOR'S NOTE.

sciousness this danger of which the ego is unaware, we obliterate the distinction between true and neurotic anxiety and are able to treat the latter as we would the former.

In the case of a true danger we develop two reactions: an affective one, the outbreak of anxiety, and action looking to protection from the danger. Presumably the same thing happens in the case of instinctual danger. We are acquainted with the instance of the purposeful coöperation of the two reactions, wherein one of them gives the signal for the initiation of the other, but we know also of a useless and inexpedient form, namely, paralysis through fear, in which the one is promulgated at the expense of the other.

There are cases in which the attributes of true and of neurotic anxiety are intermingled. The danger is known and of the real type, but the anxiety in regard to it is disproportionately great, greater than in our judgment it ought to be. It is by this excess that the neurotic element stands revealed. But these cases contribute nothing which is new in principle. Analysis shows that involved with the known reality danger is an unrecognized instinctual danger.

It would be better not to be satisfied even with reducing anxiety to danger. What is the kernel, what is the true significance, of the danger situation? Evidently it is the estimation of our strength in comparison with its magnitude, the admission of our helplessness in the face of it—of material helplessness in the case of a true danger, of psychic helplessness in that of instinctual danger. Our judgment in this regard will be guided by actual experience; whether one is mistaken in one's evaluation makes no difference to the result. Let us call our experience in a situation of helplessness of this kind a *traumatic* situation; we then have a sufficient basis for distinguishing the *traumatic* from the *danger* situation.

Now it is an important advance in self-protection when this traumatic situation of helplessness is not merely awaited but is foreseen, anticipated. Let us call the situation in which resides the cause of this anticipation the danger situation; it is in this latter that the signal of anxiety is given. What this means is: I anticipate that a situation of helplessness will come about, or the present situation reminds me of one of the traumatic experiences which I have previously undergone. Hence I will anticipate this trauma; I will act as if it were already present as long as there is still time to avert it. Anxiety, therefore, is the expectation of the trauma on the one hand, and on the other, an attenuated repetition of it. The two characteristics which have struck us with regard to anxiety have therefore a different origin: its relation to expectation pertains to the danger situation, its indefiniteness and objectlessness to the traumatic situation of helplessness which is anticipated in the danger situation.

Having developed this series: anxiety—danger—helplessness (trauma), we may summarize the matter as follows: The danger situation is the recognized, remembered and anticipated situation of helplessness. Anxiety is the original reaction to helplessness in the traumatic situation, which is later reproduced as a call for help in the danger situation. The ego, which has experienced the trauma passively, now actively repeats an attenuated reproduction of it with the idea of taking into its own hands the directing of its course. We know that the child behaves in such a manner towards all impressions which he finds painful, by reproducing them in play; through this method of transition from passivity to activity the child attempts to cope psychically with its impressions and experiences. If this is what is meant by "abreacting a trauma," no objection can be made to it. But the crux of the matter is the initial displacement of the anxiety reaction from its origin in the situation of helplessness to the anticipation of the latter, the danger situation. There then ensue the further displacements from the danger itself to that which occasions the danger, namely, object loss and the modifications thereof already mentioned.

"Spoiling" young children has the undesirable result that the danger of object loss—the object being the protection against all situations of helplessness—is overemphasized in comparison with all other dangers. It therefore encourages persistence in that childhood state of which both motor and psychic helplessness is characteristic.

We have so far had no occasion to regard true anxiety differently from neurotic anxiety. We know the difference between them; a real danger is one which threatens from some external object, neurotic danger from an instinctual demand. In so far as this instinctual demand is a piece of reality, neurotic anxiety as well may be considered as founded on reality. We have understood that the seemingly extremely intimate relation between anxiety and neurosis derives from the fact that the ego protects itself against an instinctual danger in the same manner as against an external reality danger, but that in consequence of an imperfection of the psychic ap-

paratus this defensive activity eventuates in neurosis. We have become convinced also that instinctual
demands often become an (internal) danger only
because of the fact that their gratification would
bring about an external danger—because, therefore, this internal danger represents an external one.

On the other hand, the external (reality) danger
must have undergone internalization if it is to become significant for the ego; its relation to a situation of helplessness which has been lived through
must be recognized.[1] An instinctive recognition of
dangers threatening from without does not seem to
have been among Nature's gifts to man, save to a
very moderate degree. Small children are always doing things which endanger their lives, and for that
reason alone cannot do without the protecting object. In relation to the traumatic situation, against
which one is helpless, external and internal danger,
reality danger and instinctual demand, coincide.
Whether in the one case the ego experience a grief

[1] It may also be quite often the case that in a danger situation
which is correctly assessed as such a modicum of instinctual anxiety is superadded to the reality anxiety. The instinctual demand
from the gratification of which the ego shrinks back would then
be the masochistic one, the destructive impulse turned against
the subject's own person. Perhaps this superadded element explains the case of the anxiety reaction becoming excessive and
inexpedient, paralyzing. The fear of high places might have this
origin; its hidden feminine significance is suggestive of masochism.

which will not be assuaged, or in the other a pent-up need incapable of gratification, the economic situation is in both cases the same and motor helplessness finds expression in psychic helplessness.

The enigmatic phobias of early childhood deserve mention once again at this point. Certain of them—the fear of being alone, of the dark, of strangers—we can understand as reactions to the danger of object loss; with regard to others—fear of small animals, thunderstorms, etc.—there is the possibility that they represent the atrophied remnants of an innate preparedness against reality dangers such as is so well developed in other animals. It is the part of this archaic heritage having to do with object loss which alone has utility for man. If such childhood phobias become fixed, grow more intense, and persist into a later period of life, analysis demonstrates that their content has become connected with instinctual demands, has become the representative of internal dangers also.

C. Anxiety, Grief and Mourning

So little is known of the psychology of the emotions that the diffident remarks which follow may bespeak critical indulgence. It is at the point immediately to be referred to that the problem confronts us. We were forced to the conclusion that anxiety is the reaction to the danger of object loss. Now we already know of a reaction to object loss—namely, mourning. Therefore the question is, when do we have the one, when the other? With regard to mourning, with which we have dealt on a previous occasion,[1] one of its characteristics remained completely obscure—its especial painfulness. That separation from the object is painful seems sufficiently self-evident. But the problem is more complicated; thus: When does separation from the object give rise to anxiety, when to mourning, and when merely perhaps to grief?

Let us say at once that there is no prospect of supplying an answer to these questions. We shall resign ourselves to marking out certain boundary lines and discovering a few suggestions.

Our point of departure shall once again be the one situation which we believe we understand, that of the infant who sees a strange person in place of his mother. He then manifests the anxiety which we have interpreted as due to the danger of object loss. But the situation is more complicated than this and merits a more detailed discussion. As to the in-

[1] See *Mourning and Melancholia,* Collected Papers, Vol. IV.

fant's anxiety there is, to be sure, no doubt, but his facial expression and the fact of his crying lead one to suppose that in addition he feels pain. It seems as though in him something were fused together which later will be separated. He is not yet able to distinguish temporary absence from permanent loss; when he fails to see his mother on a given occasion, he behaves as though he would never see her again, and it requires repeated consoling experiences before he learns that such a disappearance on his mother's part is usually followed by her reappearance. The mother promotes this knowledge, so important to him, by playing with him the familiar game of covering her face and then to his joy revealing it again. Thus he is enabled, as it were, to experience longing without an accompaniment of despair.

The situation in which he misses his mother is not, owing to his miscomprehension, a danger situation for him but a traumatic one, or, more correctly, it is a traumatic one if he experiences at that juncture a need which his mother ought to gratify; it changes into a danger situation when this need is not immediate. The initial cause of anxiety, which the ego itself introduces, is therefore loss of perception of the object, which becomes equated with loss of the object. Loss of love does not yet enter into the situation. Later on, experience teaches that the object may continue to be present but may have become angry with the child, and now loss of love on the part of the object becomes a new and far more enduring danger and occasion for anxiety.

The traumatic situation of missing the mother differs in one crucial respect from the traumatic situation of birth. On that occasion there was no object present who could be missed. Anxiety was still the only reaction which took place. Subsequent thereto, repeated situations in which gratification was experienced have created out of the mother the object who is the recipient, when a need arises, of an intense cathexis, a cathexis which we may call "longingful." It is to this innovation that the reaction of grief is referable. Grief is therefore the reaction specific to object loss, anxiety to the danger which this object loss entails, or, by a further displacement, to the danger of object loss itself.

Of pain, likewise, we know very little. Its only certain meaning derives from the fact that pain—primarily and as a rule—occurs if a stimulus impinging on the periphery breaks through the defenses that oppose stimuli of excessive strength and hence acts like a continuous instinctual stimulus against

which otherwise efficacious muscular activity such
as serves to remove the stimulated region from the
stimulus remains powerless. If the pain does not
originate from a point on the skin but from an internal organ, this does not alter the situation in
any way; it is only that a bit of the internal periphery
has replaced the external. The child has obviously
occasion to experience pain of this kind which is independent of his experiencing of needs. This mode
of origin of pain seems to have very little in common with the loss of an object, however, and further,
the factor of peripheral stimulation, essential in the
case of pain, is entirely lacking in the child's situation of longing. And it certainly cannot be without significance that language has created the concept of inward, of psychic, pain, and has equated
the sensations attendant upon object loss with physical pain.[1]

In the case of physical pain there arises an intense cathexis, which may be termed narcissistic, of
the painful region of the body—a cathexis which
increases progressively and which acts upon the ego
in a so to speak evacuative manner. It is a familiar
fact that when we feel pain in the internal organs

---

[1] That is, by using the same word (*Schmerz*) for both.—TRANS-
LATOR'S NOTE.

we experience spatial and other impressions of these organs which otherwise would not be registered in consciousness at all. Furthermore, the remarkable fact that the most intense physical pain fails of its full effect (here one may not say, "remains unconscious") when we are distracted by some different interest is to be explained on the ground of the concentration of the cathexis upon the psychic representative of the painful body area. Now it is in this point that the analogy seems to consist which has allowed the transference of the sensation of pain to the mental sphere. The intense and, owing to its unappeasability, ever-increasing longingful cathexis of the missed (lost) object creates the same economic conditions as the painful cathexis of the injured body area, and makes it possible to disregard the peripheral determination of the physical pain. The transition from physical pain to psychic corresponds to the change from narcissistic to object-cathexis. The idea of the object, highly cathected out of need, plays the rôle of the body area cathected by increased stimulation. The continuous and uninhibitable character of the cathectic process brings about the same state of psychic helplessness. If the unpleasurable sensation which then arises bears the specific stamp, not necessitating more exact description, of pain, instead of being expressed in the form of anxiety, the obvious thing is to hold responsible for this a factor which has heretofore been made far too little use of in our efforts at explanation—namely, the high level of cathexis and libido-binding at which these processes resulting in sensations of unpleasure take place.

We know of still another emotional reaction to object loss—namely, mourning. Its elucidation, however, does not involve any additional difficulties. Mourning originates under the influence of reality testing, which demands categorically that one must part from the object because the object no longer exists. Now it is the task of mourning to carry out this retreat from the object in all the situations in which the object was the recipient of an intense cathexis. The painful character of this separation accords with the explanation just given—that is, it is explained by the intense and unrealizable longingful cathexis of the object during the reproduction of the situations in which the tie to the object has to be dissolved.

Index

Abasia, 15
"Abreaction," 123, 124, 141, 150
"Actual" neuroses, 51, 107, 108, 140
Adler, Alfred, 122
Affect, "transformation of," 20
Agoraphobia, 50, 82, 83, 111, 112
Ambivalence
    conflict due to, 38, 41
    mechanisms of resolving, 38, 40, 80, 134
    in compulsion neurosis, 57
    dealt with by "isolation," 72
Anorexia, 14
Anticathexis, 133 *et seq.*
    external, and repression, 136
    in compulsion neurosis, 134, 136, 145
    in hysteria, 134, 135, 145
    internal, and regression, 136
    in the phobias, 136
Anxiety
    ——, grief and mourning, 153 *et seq.*
    —— hysteria, 53
    and inhibition, 13
    and symptom formation, 111
    as an affective signal of danger, 88, 113, 142, 147, 148
    as an attenuated repetition of the trauma, 150

Anxiety, *continued*
    as a cause of repression, 50-52
    as characteristic of probably all organisms, 93
    as an efferent process, 91
    as occupying pride of place relative to other affects, 120, 121
    as a product of or the reaction to psychic helplessness, 101, 108, 149, 150
    as a reaction to the danger which object loss entails, 156
    as a reaction to loss of the object's love, 110
    as a reaction to loss or separation, 88, 102, 108, 110, 151, 154
    as a reaction to perception of the absence of the object, 99, 110
    as a response to situations which should have ceased to evoke it, 120
    as a signal for influencing the pleasure-pain mechanism, 105
    as the central problem of neurosis, 111
    as the expectation of the trauma, 150